A scene from the Vineyard Theater production of "Raised in Captivity." Set design

Photo by Carol Rosegg

# RAISED IN CAPTIVITY

## BY NICKY SILVER

DRAMATISTS
PLAY SERVICE
INC.

2

RAISED IN CAPTIVITY was produced by The Vineyard Theater (Douglas Aibel, Artistic Director; Jon Nakagowa, Managing Director) by special arrangement with Mark Anderson, in New York City, on February 28, 1995. It was directed by David Warren; the set design was by James Youmans; the costume design was by Teresa Snider-Stein; the lighting design was by Donald Holder; the sound design and original music was by John Gromada; the production manager was Mark Lorenzen and the production stage manager was Christopher de Camillis. The cast was as follows:

SEBASTIAN BLISS ................................................ Peter Frechette
BERNADETTE DIXON .................................... Patricia Clarkson
KIP DIXON ............................................................... Brian Kerwin
HILLARY MACMAHON, MIRANDA BLISS ....... Leslie Ayvazian
DYLAN TAYLOR SINCLAIR, ROGER ................ Anthony Rapp

# CHARACTERS

SEBASTIAN BLISS, early thirties

BERNADETTE DIXON, early thirties, Sebastian's sister

KIP DIXON, mid-thirties, Bernadette's husband

HILLARY MACMAHON, early forties, Sebastian's doctor

DYLAN TAYLOR SINCLAIR, early twenties, a convict

ROGER, early twenties (played by the same actor as Dylan)

MIRANDA BLISS, forties (played by the same actress as Hillary) Bernadette's and Sebastian's mother

# ACT ONE

"Bread and Water"

# ACT TWO

"Forty Dollars and a New Suit"

# AUTHOR'S NOTE

I have seldom enjoyed anything as much as working on the original production of RAISED IN CAPTIVITY. This was due not just to the personalities involved, but because we all had an innate understanding of what we were making. RAISED IN CAPTIVITY has its "absurdist" turns. It has scenes of broad comedy and big punchlines abutting passages of solemn stillness. But all of us understood that these characters are real human beings. They are genuine, sometimes tragic figures trapped at times in hilarious absurdity. They are not caricatures, which is not say they aren't funny — but their humor comes from neurosis and despair. I mention this because I have seen actors, so often, make the mistake of deciding "this is broad; I know what this is." Broad behavior must be rooted in strong need. And if the play is to make sense actors must be willing to eschew their comic masks at times and let the play breath.

I'd like to extend my sincerest thanks those who helped nurture RAISED IN CAPTIVITY. They include: Doug Aibel, Jon Nakagowa and everyone at the Vineyard Theater; George Lane and Mary Meagher, my agents (listed — please note — alphabetically); Mark Anderson; Tim Sanford; Bruce Whitacre; John Guare; Peter Manning, Leslie Urdang and Max Meyer of New York Stage and Film; Alma Cuervo and John Slattery, who did the workshop; my good friend James Bart Upchurch III, who helped me learn a bit about prison and a good deal more about myself; my dear friend Chuck Coggins, witness to some of the most neurotic behavior ever!; the extraordinary cast listed in this edition—each one of them is simply brilliant and generous; and David Warren, whom I also call my close friend and who understands theater and everything perfectly. Thanks.

# RAISED IN CAPTIVITY

## ACT ONE

### "Bread and Water"

### Scene 1

*A cemetery. A pool of light comes up on Sebastian Bliss, seated on a bench, reading a book. He addresses the audience.*

SEBASTIAN.    On Tuesday, my mother was taking a shower, when the shower-head, which was obviously loose to begin with, flew away from the wall and, propelled by water pressure, hit her in the head and killed her. Odd, as I knew her to be a person who, primarily took baths. I hadn't seen my mother in several years, although we spoke on the phone, on birthdays and Christmas. I left home when I was sixteen. I turned my back on everything and went off to pursue my education. My mother said, "Good luck," and my father said nothing, having died under mysterious circumstances before I was born. There were no pictures of him in our home and we never said his name. When asked about him, my mother abruptly changed the subject. Or, occasionally feigned sudden deafness. In any event, I walked away from servants and swimming pools to live on complimentary peanuts and cashews in cocktail lounges. *(Pause. He looks over his shoulder.)* My sister is watching me. From behind that tree. *(He continues reading. His light dims. A light comes up on Bernadette and Kip Dixon in another part of the cemetery. She is overwrought.)*

7

BERNADETTE.   I don't know what to do.

KIP.   I don't think I like it here.

BERNADETTE.   What?

KIP.   It's *too* peaceful.

BERNADETTE.   Naturally it's peaceful. It's a cemetery. Everyone's dead. Did you expect picnicking families frolicking between graves?

KIP.   That would be nice. We should have a picnic. Let's go.

BERNADETTE.   What are you talking about?

KIP.   What's the name of this place?

BERNADETTE.   Pleasant Meadows.

KIP.   It's creepy.

BERNADETTE.   Please don't be disagreeable, Kip. Not today. Not now.

KIP.   Sorry.

BERNADETTE.   If I'm going to talk to him, it should be now. He should come back to the house. Don't you think? People will think it's odd. People expect him. Why should I talk to him? Why doesn't he come over and talk to me? He saw me. I know he did. Do you think I should go over to him?

KIP.   I suppose.

BERNADETTE.   You think so?

KIP.   He's your brother.

BERNADETTE.   We never speak. I never see him. I haven't seen him in — He looks older.

KIP.   He looks nice.

BERNADETTE.   Do I look older?

KIP.   Older than what?

BERNADETTE.   Older than I did.

KIP.   When?

BERNADETTE.   Forget it. Why doesn't he come over here!? I hate this dress. Do I look fat?

KIP.   I like that dress.

BERNADETTE.   What does that mean?

KIP.   You look lovely.

BERNADETTE.   Do I look fat!?

KIP.   You're not fat.

BERNADETTE.   Do I *look* fat!?

KIP.   No.

BERNADETTE.   I feel bloated. I feel all puffed up.

KIP.   You're very thin.

BERNADETTE.   I've been thinner.

KIP.   When?

BERNADETTE.   Of course I've been fatter too. I wish I'd known. I wish I'd had some warning. I would've dieted. I would've *fasted.* I hate seeing people! I hate seeing cousins and uncles and aunts. Cousin Paul was always so dashing. He looks like a helium balloon. God, I'm water logged. I feel like crying!

KIP.   Please don't.

BERNADETTE.   Why should I be nervous? There's nothing to be nervous about. *(General lighting comes up, revealing Sebastian as he was. Bernadette and Kip approach him.)* Sebastian?

SEBASTIAN.   Bernadette?

BERNADETTE.   I was afraid you wouldn't even recognize me. I think I'm heavier than the last time we saw each other. I have no idea when that was. But I think I'm heavier.

SEBASTIAN.   You look very well.

BERNADETTE.   Thank you. I seem to be eating more than usual lately. I don't seem to be able to get the food in fast enough. I don't understand it. Did you see Cousin Paul?

SEBASTIAN.   I didn't.

BERNADETTE.   Fat. Fat. Fat!

SEBASTIAN.   *(To Kip.)* Have we met?

KIP.   I'm Kip.

BERNADETTE.   This is my husband, Kip.

SEBASTIAN.   It's nice to meet you.

BERNADETTE.   You've met Kip.

SEBASTIAN.   I have?

KIP.   I think so.

SEBASTIAN.   I'm very sorry.

BERNADETTE.   Several times.

KIP.   It's all right.

BERNADETTE.   At Thanksgiving.

SEBASTIAN.   When was that?

KIP.   I don't know.

BERNADETTE.   At the wedding.

9

SEBASTIAN. What wedding?
BERNADETTE. My wedding.
SEBASTIAN. I was there.
KIP. Thank you for the andirons.
SEBASTIAN. Don't mention it.
BERNADETTE. Do you remember?
SEBASTIAN. *(To Kip.)* Did we speak?
KIP. I don't recall.
BERNADETTE. You must've said something.
SEBASTIAN. I *am* sorry.
BERNADETTE. He was the groom.
KIP. *(Sadly.)* Don't worry about it.
BERNADETTE. Kip's a dentist.
SEBASTIAN. Congratulations.
KIP. Thank you.
SEBASTIAN. It's nice to meet you, again.
KIP. I'm very sorry about your mother.
SEBASTIAN. Don't mention it.
BERNADETTE. Can you believe it?
SEBASTIAN. Yes.
BERNADETTE. It seems unreal.
KIP. *(To Sebastian.)* Do you like this place?
SEBASTIAN. Pardon me?
BERNADETTE. Can I join you? I saw you sitting here, by yourself. I saw you at the funeral home, but —
KIP. The gravestones look like teeth.
BERNADETTE. Do you mind that I came over? If you do, you can say so. you won't hurt my feelings. I'll understand. Sometimes people just want to be by themselves. I enjoy being by myself quite a bit. Other times I enjoy being with — Kip. It's wonderful to see you. I feel like it's been years. Has it been? May I sit down? You were reading. Maybe you just want to be alone. Reading can be a wonderful escape. My best friends are all characters in books. I wonder what that means? Are you glad that I came over, or would you just rather I went away?
SEBASTIAN. Please sit down, Bern. You're giving me a headache.

BERNADETTE. I'm sorry. *(Bernadette sits next to Sebastian. Kip sits on the ground.)*
KIP. Don't the headstones look like teeth?
SEBASTIAN. What does that mean?
KIP. Crooked and rotting.
SEBASTIAN. Well, I don't know —
BERNADETTE. Forget it —
KIP. They look like teeth to me. Teeth in a very old person's mouth.
BERNADETTE. Please stop talking about teeth, Kip!
KIP. I hate this place.
BERNADETTE. Why are you sitting on the ground?
KIP. Don't bury me here.
BERNADETTE. Hmmm. So, what are you reading?
SEBASTIAN. *Helter Skelter.*
BERNADETTE. I never read that.
KIP. I've read it.
SEBASTIAN. I've read it before. *(Kip looks around, becoming morose.)*
BERNADETTE. You look well. Did I say that? Are you doing well? Financially? I read that piece you wrote in *Vanity Fair.* I liked it, but I'm not sure I understood it. Is your health good?
SEBASTIAN. I have esophageal reflux.
BERNADETTE. I don't know what that is. What is that?
SEBASTIAN. It's complicated.
BERNADETTE. I'm *not* unintelligent.
SEBASTIAN. I never said you were.
BERNADETTE. You implied it.
SEBASTIAN. You inferred it.
BERNADETTE. I didn't. Kip! Did Sebastian imply that I'm stupid, or didn't he?
KIP. What?
BERNADETTE. Oh forget it.
SEBASTIAN. It's like heartburn.
BERNADETTE. What is?
SEBASTIAN. *(Losing his patience.)* Esophageal reflux.
BERNADETTE. Oh. In what way?

SEBASTIAN.   It feels like heartburn.

BERNADETTE.   I see.

SEBASTIAN.   I get it almost every night. It comes from sleeping on the wrong side.

BERNADETTE.   Of the bed?

SEBASTIAN.   Of your body.

BERNADETTE.   I meant that!

KIP.   When I die, I'd like to be thrown into the ocean.

SEBASTIAN.   Pardon?

KIP.   There's a group that does that, throws you into the ocean. I can't remember their name, but I —

BERNADETTE.   Kip *please*, I'm talking to my brother.

KIP.   Sorry.

BERNADETTE.   It was a nice service, don't you think? Not too much "God" and that sort of thing. Just enough. It's important to find a balance.

SEBASTIAN.   I suppose.

BERNADETTE.   We were lucky. It looked like rain this morning. That would've been terrible. I think the clouds were appropriate.

SEBASTIAN.   You cried beautifully.

BERNADETTE.   Thank you.

SEBASTIAN.   Very loudly.

KIP.   She's very good.

BERNADETTE.   *(Coy.)* Stop Kip.

SEBASTIAN.   She always was.

KIP.   *(To Sebastian.)* Do you cry?

SEBASTIAN.   I'm afraid not.

KIP.   *(Sadly.)* Neither do I.

SEBASTIAN.   *(To Bernadette.)* You sang well too.

BERNADETTE.   Thanks.

SEBASTIAN.   Very audibly.

KIP.   She cries a lot.

SEBASTIAN.   What was the song?

BERNADETTE.   *"This Could be the Start of Something Big."*

KIP.   Did she cry as a child?

SEBASTIAN.   I think so.

BERNADETTE.   It was her favorite.

SEBASTIAN. Was it?

BERNADETTE. You will come back to the house with us, won't you?

SEBASTIAN. I have to get back to the city.

BERNADETTE. But —

SEBASTIAN. I have an appointment.

BERNADETTE. It'll be nice.

SEBASTIAN. Maybe afterwards.

BERNADETTE. People expect you.

SEBASTIAN. I'll call you. It might be late.

BERNADETTE. Would you like to stay with us for a little while?

SEBASTIAN. No.

BERNADETTE. Kip and I have discussed it. He wouldn't mind. Would you Kip?

KIP. No.

SEBASTIAN. No thank you.

BERNADETTE. For just a little while, until the shock wears off. It was so sudden. I still can't believe it. I may never take another shower. — You can stay for a week, or a month. Whatever you like.

SEBASTIAN. I don't think so.

BERNADETTE. It'll be fun! And besides, there are things to do, things to divide. There are heirlooms and furniture and Mother's jewelry and the estate. We have plenty of room. Tell him Kip.

KIP. We have plenty of room.

BERNADETTE. It'll be just like when we were children!

SEBASTIAN. I don't want to.

BERNADETTE. *(Sweetly.)* Do you remember when we were children?

SEBASTIAN. Vaguely.

BERNADETTE. *(Slightly hostile.)* Well so do I.

KIP. They should call this place *Un*pleasant Meadow.

BERNADETTE. *(Standing.)* I think I'm going to cry again.

SEBASTIAN. I'd rather you didn't.

KIP. *(To Sebastian.)* Don't waste your breath.

BERNADETTE. I feel so awful! I'm going to cry.

SEBASTIAN. Please don't.

BERNADETTE. I can't help it.

SEBASTIAN. You cry so loudly.

BERNADETTE. I'm sorry.

KIP. You get used to it.

SEBASTIAN. Let's talk about something else — Kip, do you enjoy being a dentist?

KIP. God no.

BERNADETTE. Here it comes!

SEBASTIAN. Maybe you're going to sneeze?

BERNADETTE. I'm not.

KIP. Teeth make me sick.

SEBASTIAN. *(To Bernadette.)* People will stare.

BERNADETTE. So what? What if they do? And I don't see why people should stare anyway. My mother has just been buried! I would think some tears are called for under the circumstances!

SEBASTIAN. I don't want people to stare. I don't like being gawked at. *(Bernadette turns away and starts to sob.)*

BERNADETTE. OH GOD!! I never said good-bye! I never —

SEBASTIAN. *(To Kip.)* It makes me uncomfortable.

BERNADETTE. I never told her I loved her!

KIP. Yes you did. I heard you.

BERNADETTE. But I never meant it!! I said what I was supposed to say when I was supposed to say it! Now it's too late!

SEBASTIAN. Pull yourself together.

BERNADETTE. *(Turning to Sebastian.)* Why should I?! To please you? I'm very sorry but I can't spend my life trying to please you. It's been too many hideous years already, trying, reaching out to you — only to be spurned! Sebastian, I've tried to be a friend to you. You're my brother and I want you in my life, but I can take no more humiliation! I matter too!

SEBASTIAN. Fine.

BERNADETTE. *(Composing herself.)* I'm sorry. I am. Really. I'm just upset and so I say things, ugly things. You can't blame me. Can you? You know I love you, don't you? Don't you? I do. We only have each other now. Well you have me and I have — Kip. We're so alone! We're random, drifting orphans!!

SEBASTIAN.  We're too old to be orphans.

BERNADETTE.  We're Annie Warbucks and Oliver Twist!

SEBASTIAN.  I *have* to go.

KIP.  It was nice meeting —

BERNADETTE.  *(To Sebastian.)* You don't care, do you? You don't care one bit that she's dead. You hated her! You're completely self-absorbed. You always were. You never shared. You stay away for years at a stretch and sever your ties! You think you can erase your past and live without roots.

KIP.  *(To Sebastian.)* It was nice meeting you —

BERNADETTE.  *(Cutting him off.)* Well, Sebastian, I wasn't going to say anything, because I don't know if this is really the right place, but I think it is patently *immoral* of you to disappear from our lives and return, show up just in time to claim half of everything. You think you're entitled. I'm sorry, but I don't! Why should you be? You didn't have to deal with her. No! You have your glamorous literary friends. You sit around the Russian Tea Room all day eating blintzes and trading bon mots! You never suffered her venomous glares and the constant insults, the barrage of insults pecking away at my self-confidence. She *adored* you. You were some perfect abstract figure in the alcoholic haze of her imagination. You have a perfect life, don't you? I don't care. I have a perfect life too. — You didn't endure her epithets and the black stream of complaints about my life and my husband and my wardrobe. She hated this dress! That's why I wore it!!! So, so, so I think it is just in the worst possible taste for you to come marching up, making demands for things to which, I'm sorry, but I don't believe you're entitled! I hope I haven't hurt you. But that's how I feel.

SEBASTIAN.  I don't want anything. You can keep it all. *(Pause.)*

BERNADETTE.  Kip and I have discussed it and we would be so happy if you came for a visit. A week, say, or two. A month.

SEBASTIAN.  I *really* have to go.

BERNADETTE.  *(Mumbled.)* Why do you hate me?

SEBASTIAN.  What?

BERNADETTE.   Why do you hate me?

SEBASTIAN.   I don't hate you —

BERNADETTE.   Oh please.

SEBASTIAN.   I just have to be someplace.

BERNADETTE.   You look at me and hate shoots out of you, out of your eyes.

SEBASTIAN.   It does not.

BERNADETTE.   I'm blinded by your loathing. Rays of hate! You burn holes of hate in my flesh!

SEBASTIAN.   What do you want from me!!? *(Pause. Bernadette sits to think.)*

BERNADETTE.   Well, Sebastian, I would like, if I must be honest, I would like ... to know ... that your life is not *perfect.*

SEBASTIAN.   What?

BERNADETTE.   I would like to know that you have problems.

SEBASTIAN.   Everyone has problems.

KIP.   *(Offering an example.)* I hate teeth.

BERNADETTE.   I would like to know something — terrible. About you.

SEBASTIAN.   Why?

BERNADETTE.   It would make me feel better.

SEBASTIAN.   You're insane.

KIP.   She hasn't eaten.

BERNADETTE.   You asked me what I wanted and I told you. It would mean a great deal to me. Please. Please, Sebastian, tell me something sad. Tell me something all painful and piti-ful and embarrassing. I don't care what it is. I don't! Anything. As long as it's grim and pathetic.

SEBASTIAN.   *(Uncomfortable.)* I'm late now.

BERNADETTE.   I'm begging. Is that what it takes? I'm beg-ging you, tell me something awful about your life. Please.

SEBASTIAN.   *(Stoic.)* I'm forty-five thousand dollars in debt. I haven't sold anything since that *Vanity Fair* piece you dispar-aged. I live entirely off of credit cards. I charge my rent and my food and I pay the minimum on one card with a cash ad-vance from another. I haven't had sex in eleven years. I haven't held or kissed or cared for anyone, in anything but the most superficial way, in so long that I no longer know if

I know how. *(There is a long pause.)*
BERNADETTE.    It was *wonderful* to see you! *(Bernadette, quite at peace for once, stands and kisses Sebastian on the cheek. She extends her hand to Kip, who stands and takes it.)*
SEBASTIAN.    *(Bewildered.)* Thank you.
BERNADETTE.    Tragedy brings us together. We mustn't wait so long next time.
KIP.    It was nice meeting you. Again.
SEBASTIAN.    Likewise. *(Kip and Bernadette exit. Sebastian stands alone.)*

# Scene 2

*Hillary's office. She is seated at a desk. Sebastian is seated opposite her. He is quite anxious.*

SEBASTIAN.    I don't know how to say this. I, I'm not sure how to approach it. Um. The thing is, the thing is I've made a decision. I have. *(He shifts in his chair.)* I've been coming here, to see you, every Friday for four and a half years. It's become a habit, something I do without questioning. But this morning my mother was buried — did I mention that? She was. She died. She was killed by her shower-massage. Anyway, there, at her funeral, certain things became disturbingly clear to me. My sister was there. She sang. As you know, I've mentioned Bernadette, I think she's completely insane. For instance, our birthday parties were pageants of hysteria. My mother always gave us one party, our being twins, and every year Bernadette would have what I recognized, even then, as mini-nervous breakdowns. When we were ten, we had a clown. I'll never forget it. That was the year, I think, she slipped, irredeemably 'round the bend.

It was hot, August, and the temperature must've reached a hundred and ten in that front yard. There were about two dozen children there, none of whom I particularly liked, and none of whom were having a particularly good time. We just sat there, sad, withered children on a patch of brown, burned-up grass. My mother had, as always, planned every moment of the day with military precision. Two o'clock:  three legged races. Two fifteen:  passing oranges under our chins. At three o'clock, the entertainment arrived. A clown: Mr. Giggles. Mr. Giggles was *extremely* old. It's true that all adults seem old to small children, but Mr. Giggles would have seemed *very old* to very old people! He was old. His skin was the texture and non-color of white raisins.

In any event, Mr. Giggles made flowers spring from umbrellas and foam balls appear from behind our ears. He was maniacally cheerful, despite the fact that none of us joined in or laughed or moved. Mr. Giggles thought some singing might rouse us from our collective coma. He sang "A Hundred Bottles of Beer on the Wall." Only we were ten, so he sang "A Hundred Bottles of *Milk* on the Wall." Not very imaginative was Mr. Giggles. He sang loudly and with, what should have been infectious joy: "A hundred bottles of milk on the wall, hundred bottles of milk!" And we tried! We did. At first. All of us, I think, joined in. Mr. Giggles ran around in a desperate frenzy, wild for us to perform — but it was so hot! We made it through ninety bottles of milk on the wall and eighty bottles of milk. And then.... I could take it no more. I just stopped. I laid down, put my head on the earth and shut my eyes. Well, Mr. Giggles ran over and knelt down and sang RIGHT at me, loud, shouting more than singing really. Screaming right at me:  "EIGHTY-TWO BOTTLES OF MILK ON THE WALL! EIGHTY-TWO BOTTLES OF MILK!" I refused to stir. I just opened my eyes and stared at this *fascist* clown. Then another little boy stopped. Tommy Leonardo, I think. He let his head fall foreword and fell silent. Giggles leapt upon him and shrieked with rage, "EIGHTY-ONE BOTTLES OF MILK ON THE WALL! EIGHTY-ONE BOTTLES OF MILK!" Then very quickly, other children followed suit. Like spontaneous suicides, their voices fell silent. By now Mr. Giggles was in the throws of a demented fit! Running crazy from child to child, screaming, spit flying out of him, sweat spraying off of him.— But he would not give up!

By now, no one was singing, except for my sister, who would participate in this deranged duet at any cost! I watched as Giggles flapped his arms like spastic birds and lost the count completely: "FIFTY-TWO BOTTLES OF MILK ON THE WALL! FORTY-EIGHT BOTTLES OF MILK!" And then he fell over in a sad, wet, broken pencil heap. *(Pause.)*

The silence was palpable. My sister, abandoned, looked at me. "He's dead," I whispered. Bernadette shrieked and ran, in horror, from the yard and into the street, where a bread truck swerved to avoid her and ran, head-long, into a mammoth oak tree, shaking from its perch, our cat, which fell to an ugly, bloody death, impaled by the truck's antenna and splattered on the windshield. *(Pause.)*

Of course, Mr. Giggles had had a stroke, but he lived. Still Bernadette cried for a week and refused solid food until she passed out one day from malnutrition and had to be taken to the hospital, so heavy was her burden of guilt for the death of our cat. And to this day she has a neurotic relationship with food, for which she blames me, no matter how irrational. Because she *is* irrational. And yet this morning, as she walked away from me, on the cemetery lawn, I couldn't help being jealous of her. She's insane, obviously, and unhappy, I think. But she certainly participates! She clearly feels things. I think I ought to have felt something today! Grief, anger, joy — something! But no. And she has someone in her life — no one I would pick, but someone! While I, on the other hand, have been *sitting* here every Friday for four and a half years and I'm about to celebrate my eleventh anniversary of physical and emotional celibacy.

Simon has been dead for eleven years, Dr. MacMahon, and I'm still waiting. I don't even remember any longer if I loved him. I remember thinking I did, but there's got to be a difference. Doesn't there? I have no real contact with anyone, including myself. There is my convict — But the point is this: I don't seem to be making any progress. I don't mean to criticize. It's not a matter of blame, but I'll take all the blame if you want. But, God, I am inertia given human form! And this what I suddenly understood this morning: I have to try something else. This just isn't working. So with my finances in their current state of decrepitude, and as I'm making no headway, not an *iota* of progress, I feel it's time for me to stop. Coming here. I think I should terminate my therapy.

HILLARY. I love you.

SEBASTIAN. What?

HILLARY. I know that was very hard for you to say.

SEBASTIAN. Thank you.

HILLARY. And I love you.

SEBASTIAN. I don't understand.

HILLARY. I don't want to make you uncomfortable.

SEBASTIAN. Then why say a thing like that?

HILLARY. I don't mean I'm *in love* with you. I mean I love you.

SEBASTIAN. This is extremely irritating.

HILLARY. Emotion embarrasses you.

SEBASTIAN. I'm trying to tell you I think this should be our last session.

HILLARY. Do you think it's wrong for me to love you?

SEBASTIAN. I do. Yes. I would say so. Yes.

HILLARY. How can it be? Human beings love each other. What could be more wonderful?

SEBASTIAN. We're not human beings. You're my doctor.

HILLARY. You're a part of my life and I care about you.

SEBASTIAN. Well stop it. Stop it right now.

HILLARY. Don't let my feelings hurt you. I don't want to have sex with you. I don't have romantic feelings, I have ethics. Anyway, I know you're homosexual.

SEBASTIAN. Maybe I'm not. Maybe I was hasty! It's possible that all of my encounters, longings and sexual dreams have been an aberration, and that's why I seem so stuck.

HILLARY. Don't you love me?

SEBASTIAN. No.

HILLARY. Just a little bit?

SEBASTIAN. No.

HILLARY. A teeny-tiny, itsy-bitsy, little bit?

SEBASTIAN. No.

HILLARY. You're a homosexual.

SEBASTIAN.  Because I don't love you?

HILLARY.  Because you are.

SEBASTIAN.  I *like* you.

HILLARY.  Wake up and smell the coffee.

SEBASTIAN.  Sort of, sometimes.

HILLARY.  You are what you are. I am what I am. Ad infinitum!

SEBASTIAN.  Do you see any progress? Answer me that. Be honest. I ask myself, what makes me happy? And the only thing I can come up with is a once-a-month letter from a murderer — I think I'm —

HILLARY.  What if I didn't charge you so much?

SEBASTIAN.  No.

HILLARY.  What if I didn't charge you at all?

SEBASTIAN.  I'd just feel guilty.

HILLARY.  You wouldn't! You don't feel things! That's why you come.

SEBASTIAN.  I'd feel that.

HILLARY.  We could try it and see! If it bothers you, I'll charge you more than I do now.

SEBASTIAN.  No. *(Pause.)*

HILLARY.  Tell me, are you going to see someone else?

SEBASTIAN.  Wha — I don't know. I haven't thought about it.

HILLARY.  Have you started with another doctor already?

SEBASTIAN.  No.

HILLARY.  You can be honest with me.

SEBASTIAN.  I am.

HILLARY.  Why don't you just admit it?

SEBASTIAN.  Admit what?

HILLARY.  You're seeing someone else!!

SEBASTIAN.  I feel you're taking this personally. — I had a very interesting dream last night.

HILLARY.  I don't care about your dreams! I don't give a shit about your dreams! I'm not a Freudian! Have I ever asked about your dreams? What kind of game is this? How long have you been seeing this "other" doctor? A week? A month? I have a right to know. I think you owe me that much after the decades of sitting here, sifting through the morass of your neurotic mumbles.

SEBASTIAN.  I don't think I believe in psychiatry.

HILLARY.  *(Turning away, dissolving.)* This is so very typical. I should've expected this. Everyone leaves!

SEBASTIAN.  What?

HILLARY.  Everyone leaves me! I lie in bed at night and hear the sound of doors slamming. Everyone goes. I'm a bad person.

SEBASTIAN.  I was hoping to avoid a confrontation.

HILLARY.  I am. I am a very, very bad person.

SEBASTIAN.  There are no "bad" people.

HILLARY.  Of course there are, and I'm one. I stink.

SEBASTIAN.  There are unhappy people; people with problems.

HILLARY.  I'm happy when bad things happen to people I hate.

SEBASTIAN.  That makes you human, not bad.

HILLARY.  When I was a little girl I was best friends with Monica Taylor. She got mono. I had a party!

SEBASTIAN.  You were a child.

HILLARY.  Balloons, favors, you name it, the works.

SEBASTIAN.  You're an adult now.

HILLARY.  Oh people don't change!! The quality of our humanity is genetic. Immutable from birth.

SEBASTIAN.  How can you think that? You're a psychiatrist.

HILLARY.  *(Correcting him.)* I'm a *psychologist.*

SEBASTIAN.  Human potential is limitless.

HILLARY.  Why did my husband walk out?!

SEBASTIAN.  I didn't even know you were married.

HILLARY.  *(A bit frenzied now.)* I thought he was happy. He looked happy. We never fought. He was a beautiful man. We met in graduate school. He never gave the slightest indication that anything was rotten and falling apart from the inside. He read a lot and smiled quietly. I consider that a lie. His calm was a deception as far as I'm concerned. — The girl who worked the coffee counter at Dean & DeLuca's was *nineteen* years old! I know because I went there after he left and choked down cup after cup of some vile anisette slop, studying her the whole time. She looked like the White Rock Soda pixie! I bet she had no pubic hair!

SEBASTIAN. Did you ever read *The Executioner's Song?*

HILLARY. No. — One day I came home and there was a note saying he'd found his future in the eyes of some barely post-pubescent coffee vendor, and the great pattern of my life continues! I'm simply bad! Everyone leaves! I'm a burning building. I'm the Titanic!! My parents never wanted me and they counted the minutes till they could escape!!

SEBASTIAN. I thought you said once your parents were hit by a car?

HILLARY. But they were leaving at the time! They were moving to another state, an *undisclosed* state! *I have anti-magnetism!!*

SEBASTIAN. *(Embarrassed.)* I think you're charming. *(Pause.)*

HILLARY. So. You'll continue our work?

SEBASTIAN. No.

HILLARY. Please?

SEBASTIAN. No.

HILLARY. *(Sincere, pathetic.)* How can you, how can you do this?

SEBASTIAN. I don't think it's helping and I don't think it's healthy.

HILLARY. I have a Ph.D. I know what's healthy.

SEBASTIAN. Dr. MacMahon —

HILLARY. Hillary, please.

SEBASTIAN. Dr. MacMahon, I feel all our boundaries have dissolved.

HILLARY. Boundaries are for countries on a map, not people.

SEBASTIAN. You've told me too much about yourself. For four years you never said a thing. Occasionally you asked how I felt about something. Once you said "excuse me," after you sneezed.

HILLARY. I can talk more.

SEBASTIAN. Please don't. I know too much already. I feel all sorry for you, like you're the patient and I'm the doctor. I don't want to know your tragedies.

HILLARY. Forget I said anything.

SEBASTIAN.   It's too late.

HILLARY.   *(Sadly.)* Did I mention my dog, Scraps, died of spinal tumors?

SEBASTIAN.   Be that as it may —

HILLARY.   I loved that dog!

SEBASTIAN.   I simply cannot continue therapy with you. *(Pause. Hillary is near tears and seems to withdraw into herself.)*

HILLARY.   I feel very betrayed. And very sad. Sad all over.

SEBASTIAN.   I'm sorry.

HILLARY.   Nothing works.

SEBASTIAN.   I think I should be going.

HILLARY.   Where?

SEBASTIAN.   Away.

HILLARY.   You're ... really not ... coming back?

SEBASTIAN.   No.

HILLARY.   Don't go.

SEBASTIAN.   I'm sorry. I am.

HILLARY.   *(Simply.)* I need you.

SEBASTIAN.   I know.

HILLARY.   Please.

SEBASTIAN.   Good-bye. *(He exits. There is a pause. Hillary weeps, her head in her hands. Then, abruptly, she places her hand on the desk and grabs a letter opener. She stabs her hand.)*


# Scene 3

*The Dixon living room, or a fragment of it. It is the middle of the night. Kip is looking out the window. After a moment, Bernadette enters, wearing a bathrobe.*

BERNADETTE.   Kip?

KIP.   Did I wake you?

BERNADETTE.   What are you doing?

KIP.   It's a beautiful night. The clouds have passed.

BERNADETTE.   I woke up and the bed was empty. I didn't know where you were.

KIP.   I didn't mean to wake you.

BERNADETTE.   I got scared.

KIP.   Come look at this.

BERNADETTE.   Is something out there?

KIP.   Come here.

BERNADETTE.   I'm tired. It's been a very long, trying day.

KIP.   *(Turning away.)* Then go to bed.

BERNADETTE.   Are you coming?

KIP.   No.

BERNADETTE.   What are you looking at? *(She goes to the window.)*

KIP.   The moon.

BERNADETTE.   The moon? The moon, Kip? You're looking at the moon?

KIP.   Isn't it beautiful?

BERNADETTE.   It looks dirty.

KIP.   What would you call that color?

BERNADETTE.   *(Exasperated.)* White?

KIP.   No, I don't think so. It's definitely not white.

BERNADETTE.   Who cares?

KIP.   Ecru, maybe. Or eggshell!

BERNADETTE.   It's a big, dirty circle in the sky. Come back to bed.

KIP.   Something happened today!

BERNADETTE.   It's not that I'm not fascinated —

KIP.   Listen to me.

BERNADETTE.   Although, I'm not.

KIP.   Do you realize that I never knew anyone who died before? It's true. My whole life, I never knew anyone who died. Isn't that startling?

BERNADETTE.   I don't understand.

KIP.   Did you know you're going to die? I didn't! I mean I had the information, tucked away in some remote corner of my brain, but seeing your mother, lifeless, still — seeing someone I didn't even like as an object made my own death a very tangible entity.

BERNADETTE.   Everyone's going to die! Everyone who's born will die.

KIP.   That's a very bleak point of view, Bernadette.

BERNADETTE.   Life is finite. Thank God.

KIP.   *(With great importance.)* I don't want to be a dentist.

BERNADETTE.   *(Stunned, then.)* No one WANTS to be a dentist!

KIP.   I don't even know why I became one.

BERNADETTE.   For the same reason as everyone else! You didn't have the grades for medical school.

KIP.   Do you know what teeth are?

BERNADETTE.   That's a rhetorical question, I assume.

KIP.   They're millstones around my neck.

BERNADETTE.   They are?

KIP.   Yes.

BERNADETTE.   Teeth?

KIP.   They're dragging me down, into a vat of dire ugliness.

BERNADETTE.   Teeth?

KIP.   I look into mouths all day, and if I felt anything I'd burst into tears. I never mentioned it because I try to be positive.

BERNADETTE.   Try harder.

KIP.   I spend my life staring into gaping, gagging crypts filled with blood and drool.

BERNADETTE.   That's very descriptive.

KIP.   *(Excited.)* I used to think I could make the mouth my canvass. I thought I could create the universe in miniature. But there is no poetry in teeth. When I was a child I saw things! I went to the museum with my mother. She dragged me from room to room, whispering into my ear the stories of the saints in the paintings. When I could, I ran off and found a room with a bench in the middle. I curled up and fell asleep. Then I opened my eyes. I saw a painting: *The City Rises* by Botcionni. It was beautiful, a scene of chaos with fire and horses and people in panic made up of a million splatters of color. And I stared at it. I studied it. And the colors came alive! Do you understand?

BERNADETTE.   You had a dream.

KIP.   I didn't! I don't know what it was, but it wasn't a dream! I told my father about it, that night at dinner. He broke all my crayons and lined the garbage with my drawing paper. He thought God was dead and I was proof.

BERNADETTE. I've lost the thread.

KIP. He taught me *not to see.*

BERNADETTE. What's the point of this!?

KIP. *(After a moment, simply.)* Do you love me, Bernadette?

BERNADETTE. Yes.

KIP. We're partners, aren't we?

BERNADETTE. Yes. Can we please go to bed?

KIP. *(Grandiose.)* I'm going to be a painter! I want to learn to see again. I think it's possible.

BERNADETTE. That's what this is all about?

KIP. Don't belittle my rebirth!

BERNADETTE. Fine. Paint if you want. Paint until your arms fall off.

KIP. I mean full time.

BERNADETTE. Pardon me?

KIP. I've looked into my last mouth.

BERNADETTE. You can't be serious!

KIP. You said you loved me. We're partners.

BERNADETTE. *(In disbelief.)* You're not going to work?

KIP. I'm going to work. I'm going to paint!

BERNADETTE. What kind of work is that?

KIP. Work worth doing. We don't need the money. We have your mother's now, and —

BERNADETTE. Oh my God.... Oh God. You're just —

KIP. Think of possibilities, Bernadette. You have no imagination.

BERNADETTE. I'm going to cry.

KIP. Do you want to go on like this for the rest of our lives?

BERNADETTE. Yes!

KIP. I want something else. You won't get what you don't want. I want a different kind of life.

BERNADETTE. I DON'T! There's nothing wrong with my life the way it is! I'm going to bed! I'd like to pretend this never happened. We never had this conversation.

KIP. Don't be angry. This is wonderful!

BERNADETTE. I think it's pretty goddamn terrible! I woke

27

up this morning next to my husband, now — who are you?!

KIP. I'm me.

BERNADETTE. You are not! I don't want to talk about it.

KIP. I hoped you'd understand.

BERNADETTE. We'll talk about it in the morning.

KIP. I hoped you'd be happy.

BERNADETTE. I'm going to bed. *(Kip takes her hand.)*

KIP. Look at me.

BERNADETTE. *(Angry.)* What?

KIP. Everything looks new to me.

BERNADETTE. I'm tired. *(He touches her face.)*

KIP. I've never seen you at all. *(He takes her hand. She turns to leave. He doesn't release her.)*

BERNADETTE. Let go of me.

KIP. Your eyes.

BERNADETTE. It's late.

KIP. It's morning.

BERNADETTE. Please.

KIP. Your hair.

BERNADETTE. It's dirty.

KIP. It's perfect.

BERNADETTE. Let go.

KIP. You're beautiful.

BERNADETTE. I'm not.

KIP. To me.

BERNADETTE. You have ...

KIP. You are.

BERNADETTE. Really lost your mind. *(He kisses her. It quickly becomes passionate and the sink to the floor, making love. Fadeout.)*

## Scene 4

*Sebastian enters a pool of light, carrying a letter. He addresses the audience.*

SEBASTIAN. I've received a letter from Dylan. I've never met Dylan — I read a book about him, detailing his case — sev-

28

eral years ago and I was deeply moved, by his plight. And his sense of humor. He has a very sharp wit for a convicted felon. Anyway, I wrote and told him so. He answered my letter and we've corresponded ever since. When he was nineteen, Dylan was convicted of first degree murder, with dubious evidence, and sentenced to death in the gas chamber. When he was twenty-two, his sentence was altered, to that of life in prison, meaning he'll be locked away for another thirty or thirty-five years. We've never met and, although I'm tempted, I plan on never seeing him. *(Sebastian reads from the letter.)* "Dear Sebastian, *(A second pool of light comes up on Dylan wearing prison coveralls. He speaks with a clipped, mid-western/southern accent and looks straight ahead as he "recites" the letter. Sebastian remains focused on the page.)*

DYLAN. "First of all, let me thank you for the money order and the clipping. I've never read *Vanity Fair* and I truly enjoyed your article, although I must admit, I do not think I really understood it all. I have finally been transferred out of the factory. My new job is that of clerk/typist, which is another example of good prison management, as I can neither type nor clerk. To answer your first question, we make wine by taking a gallon of orange juice from the kitchen, adding yeast and letting it sit for a week or two. It's not bad, really. It tastes pretty much like Mad Dog 20/20 Orange Jubilee —"

SEBASTIAN. *(Looking at Dylan.)* Dylan?

DYLAN. *(Looking at Sebastian.)* What?

SEBASTIAN. There are things I want to ask you.

DYLAN. Ask.

SEBASTIAN. I can't seem to write them down.

DYLAN. Why not?

SEBASTIAN. I'm afraid the answers are none of my business. I'm afraid of violating the boundaries of our relationship.

DYLAN. Boundaries are for countries on a map, not human beings.

SEBASTIAN. That sounds familiar. I'm afraid you'll think I'm judging you. But the answers don't matter. I'm just curious.

DYLAN. If the answers don't matter, why are you curious?

SEBASTIAN. That's a very good question.

DYLAN.  I thought you would think so. *(They return to their "positions;" Dylan looking forward, Sebastian reading.)* "Secondly, yes. The toilet is just right here, in the cell. And no, there are no curtains or dividers or anything. So true, everyone can see you take a dump. But that is something you get used to pretty quickly. And really, I do not think it would be possible to 'hold it in' for thirty years. Besides, I am sure you would get an impacted bowel —"

SEBASTIAN.  *(Looking at Dylan.)* Do I look like what you thought I'd look like?

DYLAN.  *(Looking at Sebastian.)* I didn't think about it one way or the other.

SEBASTIAN.  Is prison like, well, what I assume it's like?

DYLAN.  What do you assume it's like?

SEBASTIAN.  Are there drugs everywhere?

DYLAN.  Yes.

SEBASTIAN.  Is everyone raped all the time?

DYLAN.  No.

SEBASTIAN.  Do you have friends?

DYLAN.  Of course. I'm very likable.

SEBASTIAN.  True.

DYLAN.  I am the wittiest guy on my cell block. People like me.

SEBASTIAN.  I like you. *(A third pool of light comes up on Bernadette.)*

BERNADETTE.  I simply cannot *fathom* the appeal of this relationship.

DYLAN.  Who's that?

SEBASTIAN.  That's my sister, Bernadette.

DYLAN.  It's nice to meet you.

BERNADETTE.  Don't talk to me.

SEBASTIAN.  Don't be rude.

BERNADETTE.  Don't tell me what to do!

DYLAN.  Don't argue.

BERNADETTE.  Don't interfere!

SEBASTIAN.  Don't speak to him.

BERNADETTE.  Don't you understand that this is a fixation bordering on the perverse? How can you be friends with him?

And don't think I don't know you spend a small fortune on books and presents —

DYLAN. *(To Sebastian.)* Thank you for the copy of *In Cold Blood.*

SEBASTIAN. Don't mention it.

BERNADETTE. Sebastian, you're my brother and I want you to be happy. I want you to have *someone* in your life. But you are obsessed with a convicted felon!

SEBASTIAN. Why don't you just mind your own fucking business!

BERNADETTE. I'm going to cry now. *(Bernadette's light goes out.)*

DYLAN. She seems highly-strung.

SEBASTIAN. Where was I?— Oh yes. *(Sebastian and Dylan resume their "reading" positions: Sebastian reads; Dylan looks ahead.)*

DYLAN. "Yes, Sebastian, it is true that you can send things at Christmas that you cannot send at other times of the year. You can send food. Beef jerky is a particular favorite. You can send white handkerchiefs, sneakers, radios and jewelry valued at under two-hundred dollars. But do remember, it takes a special strand of pearls to take these coveralls from day to evening —"

SEBASTIAN. *(Looking at Dylan.)* Do you miss people?

DYLAN. *(Looking at Sebastian.)* Some people.

SEBASTIAN. Your family?

DYLAN. My brothers and sister.

SEBASTIAN. Not your mother?

DYLAN. She died last year.

SEBASTIAN. I'm sorry.

DYLAN. Of a heart attack.

SEBASTIAN. Do you miss your father?

DYLAN. My father thinks I'm doomed to an eternity in "the lake of fire."

SEBASTIAN. What does that mean?

DYLAN. I don't miss him.

SEBASTIAN. Does he think you did it?

DYLAN. Do *you* think I did it?

SEBASTIAN. I don't know — *(Dylan returns to his "reading*

*position." Sebastian continues looking at Dylan.)*

DYLAN. "They're gonna turn off the lights soon, so I better sign off —"

SEBASTIAN. No —

DYLAN. "All for now,"

SEBASTIAN. Yes —

DYLAN. "Sincerely, Dylan Taylor Sinclaire." *(Dylan looks at Sebastian. Sebastian reaches out for him as Dylan's light fades out. After a moment Sebastian addresses the audience.)*

SEBASTIAN. I can't make up my mind. On one hand, I don't want to think that innocent people end up on death row. On the other hand, I don't want to believe that someone I care about, because I do, is so basically ... bad. *(Sebastian's light fades out.)*

## Scene 5

*The Dixon's living room, or a fragment of it. Kip is standing at an easel, holding a pallet and a paint brush, poised to paint. Bernadette enters and sits on a stool, striking a pose.*

BERNADETTE. We *have* to talk.

KIP. Don't move. *(He paints.)*

BERNADETTE. I'm not comfortable.

KIP. The light is very warm today.

BERNADETTE. I'm not comfortable, Kip!

KIP. All right, stretch. *(He stops painting.)*

BERNADETTE. I don't mean physically, although I mean that as well. I mean with everything. Do you understand?

KIP. *(Cheery.)* Finished? *(He resumes painting.)*

BERNADETTE. I'm not happy with my life.

KIP. Your eyes are ... are ... are ...

BERNADETTE. We never go anywhere. We never see anyone.

KIP. — your eyes are —

BERNADETTE. I hate my life. I wish I were an alcoholic.

32

KIP.    Your eyes are mud.

BERNADETTE.    I have to talk to you.

KIP.    *(Perky.)* You talk. I'll paint your bust.

BERNADETTE.    This is not what I wanted.

KIP.    Your breasts are Monet's apples.

BERNADETTE.    Not what I hoped for.

KIP.    Or Cézanne's apples.

BERNADETTE.    I feel sick.

KIP.    Someone's apples. They're apples — or lettuce!

BERNADETTE.    I want to be taken care of. I want my privacy! I want a vodka collins.

KIP.    You're a salad.

BERNADETTE.    This is some kind of punishment. That's what I think. I think I'm being punished because when I was growing up my mother worked too hard and she was angry all the time. She criticized my posture — so I prayed at night that she would die and then she did and now God's punishing me. I wanted to escape and you told me I was thin and so I loved you.

KIP.    If you keep talking, you're mouth'll be blurry.

BERNADETTE.    I DON'T CARE! I want to go shopping! I want to watch TV! I hate this stool and I hate sitting here hour after hour, day after day! I hate being a model, I'm too fat!

KIP.    You're not fat. You're thin.

BERNADETTE.    I'm not falling for that again.

KIP.    Your hands are swallows.

BERNADETTE.    WHAT THE FUCK ARE YOU TALKING ABOUT? CAN YOU HEAR YOURSELF?! ARE YOU DEAF TO THE RIDICULOUS STREAM OF BLACK SHIT THAT IS VOMITING OUT OF YOUR MOUTH?!! MY HANDS ARE NOT SPARROWS! MY HANDS ARE NOT BIRDS AND MY TITS ARE NOT APPLES!!!

KIP.    *(Correcting her.)* They're lettuce.

BERNADETTE.    LEAVES OF LETTUCE?! HEADS OF LETTUCE!? WHAT THE FUCK DOES THAT MEAN?!

KIP.    You're too literal.

BERNADETTE.    My head is spinning from paint fumes.

KIP.    I'm using acrylics.

BERNADETTE.  I HAVE DREAMS AT NIGHT THAT YOU
FALL ON A PAINT BRUSH AND *DIE!!* I DREAM YOU CUT
YOUR THROAT WITH YOUR PALLET KNIFE! — I'm sorry!
I am. I really am. I don't know what's wrong with me. This is
not how I intended this scene to go. Let's start over. I'll go
out and come back in and I'll say, "We have to talk." And you
say, "Don't move." And I'll say, "I'm not comfortable." And
maybe we can make it go better — YOU WORTHLESS SACK
OF STEAMING SHIT!! — oops! Did it again. Didn't mean
that. Swear to God. I don't understand what's wrong with me
today, MOTHER-FUCKER! PRETENTIOUS, USELESS, STINK-
ING TURD!! — shoot, damn, damn. You know I love you,
don't you?
KIP.  *(Still painting cheerily.)* Uh-huh.
BERNADETTE.  I do. I really, really, really, really, really do.
It's just that these last few months have been SO unnerving!
I used to be a calm person. All right, I wasn't a calm person.
But I was happy. Ok, ok, ok, I wasn't happy. But I was hap-
pi*er!* And I had some motor control over my mouth! But you
NEVER leave the house!! Don't you want to? I bet it's nice
out. I bet it's a lovely day. I bet the birds are singing "*Bie Mier
Bis du Sheon*" in three-part harmony.
KIP.  My days were so dreary before I saw, before I understood the journey of my life. I was an idiot marking time. A
blind man in the woods.
BERNADETTE.  EVERYTHING THAT COMES OUT OF
YOUR MOUTH IS SHIT! — I mean, tell me more — YOU
PUERILE SLAB OF STINKING PUKE! — I love you — I don't
know if I mentioned that. You entered my world and I was
sooo happy. I never had a date before you. It's true. My
mother told me the timbre of my voice gave people a rash,
so I mumbled. I never had a boyfriend. I never had a lab part-
ner in chemistry! I thought I was fat and I used to make myself vomit twice a day, then I took up reading instead. You
told me I was beautiful and I believed you. Or at least I believed you believed it. And I thought you were nice looking
and I liked that brown tweed jacket you used to wear. Do you
still think I'm beautiful?

KIP. *(Stopping, studying her.)* I do. You are. Your skin is smooth and your hair catches the sun and shatters it into a million shards of color. I love your eyes and teeth and lips and ears.
BERNADETTE. I still have that tweed jacket.
KIP. Everything is beautiful.
BERNADETTE. *(Disgruntled.)* What does that mean?
KIP. I was out walking this morning — it was dawn and you were asleep —
BERNADETTE. *(Utter disbelief.)* You have no aesthetic criteria, *at all?*
KIP. I saw flowers of every color, colors I couldn't name and shapes I couldn't describe. And then, there, by the side of the road, I came upon a horse.
BERNADETTE. A horse?
KIP. A dead horse, on the shoulder of the road. It was split open, exploded somehow. Its insides were spilling out onto the black tar of the street. Its stomach and kidneys and guts were overflowing in a puddle of blood.
BERNADETTE. *(Slightly sick.)* Please stop.
KIP. It was a deep, perfect alizarin crimson, reflecting the burnt umber of the coming sun. The organs were all shades of raw ochre and aubergine. The curves of the neck and angels of the legs, the long sloping lines of dead muscle! All of this was beautiful to me!
BERNADETTE. And you think I'm beautiful?
KIP. I do.
BERNADETTE. I see. *(Pause. She poses. He paints.)*
KIP. My world has been too small. I want to go to Africa!
BERNADETTE. I'm pregnant! *(He stares at her, dumb struck. She looks irritated.)*

# Scene 6

*Hillary steps into a pool of light and addresses the audience. She is wearing rags and the hand she stabbed previously is heavily bandaged. In her other hand, she carries a screwdriver.*

HILLARY.  We were not people of God. I believe Mother was a communist, although she enjoyed the fruits of my father's capitalism, while he sat quietly in a corner reading *Moby Dick*. I had no religion or religious training. While my little friends in school were rebelling against their structures I was free to worship Karl Marx, or Lenin, or Margaret Sanger, and encouraged to worship Freud and Jung. *(A light comes up on Dylan. He addresses the audience. Hillary is annoyed by the interruption and grows more so as the scene gets away from her.)*

DYLAN.  We were Baptist, and pretty regular about it. Now that I'm in prison, I'm a Muslim. *(A light comes up on Kip. He addresses the audience.)*

KIP.  My father was Jewish. My mother was Episcopalian. We celebrated Christmas and Hanukkah. But we pronounced it "*Ha*nukkah," not "*Cha*nukah." *(Light comes up on both Bernadette and Sebastian. They address the audience.)*

BERNADETTE and SEBASTIAN.  We went to church on Christmas and Easter, but it was just an irritation —

BERNADETTE.  Kip and I have discussed it, and we'd like it very much if you came to stay with us for a little while, after the baby comes.

SEBASTIAN.  No thank you.

BERNADETTE.  It'd be nice. You could get to know your little niece.

KIP.  Or nephew.

SEBASTIAN.  No.

BERNADETTE.  Don't you want to visit little Sydney?

SEBASTIAN.  Not particularly.

KIP.  We're not calling the baby Sydney.

BERNADETTE.   Well, we're not calling it Ruth.

KIP.   It was my father's mother's name.

BERNADETTE.   Yuk.

KIP.   I like the name Ruth.

BERNADETTE.   You're the one.

DYLAN.   *(To no one in particular.)* I like the name Ruth.

BERNADETTE.   The favorite of killers.

DYLAN.   *(Deciding.)* My Muslim name is Ruth.

SEBASTIAN, BERNADETTE, HILLARY and KIP.   What?

BERNADETTE.   *(To Sebastian.)* It'll be such fun. We have the space. We're adding a room, for the baby.

SEBASTIAN.   *(To Dylan.)* Your Muslim name is *Ruth?*

BERNADETTE.   We'd love to have you.

SEBASTIAN.   *(To Dylan.)* Are you gay?

DYLAN.   Not yet.

BERNADETTE.   *(To Kip.)* Tell him.

KIP.   *(Dreamily.)* It's always summer on Cape Horn.

BERNADETTE.   Say you'll come!

SEBASTIAN.   Leave me alone!

HILLARY.   AS I WAS SAYING!!! *(All lights go out, except for Hillary's.)* I had no God. And although, intellectually, I have always found the idea of "God," per se, rather far-fetched and revoltingly patriarchal, and *organized* religion seems, to me, to be little more than another systematic mechanism by which the plutocratic echelon controls the educational and economic underclass, it does also, obviously provide that subclass a system, with which those who feel burdened by sociologically imposed guilt can purge those feelings, and continue their lives in a clean, new, virgin state.

I went to the church near my house and told the priest that I was bad and I wanted to make a confession. I said, "Father, I am bad. I am pocked with the mark of Cain." He asked me when I last made a confession, and I told him never. He said he was unclear as to what, exactly, my sins were. And I told him that I couldn't be any clearer right now, but that my spirit was spent from shouldering a tremendous, nameless guilt. Then he asked me if I wanted to buy a chance in the church raffle. The grand prize was a micro-wave. I told him no. I wouldn't feel comfortable buying a raffle and supporting an organization that refuses to recognize women as priests. I couldn't contribute because I believe a woman has the right to control her own body. I feel condoms should be distributed in the public schools because of the AIDS plague and I don't think everyone who uses birth control pills goes to hell. He told me to get out and return only after I'd rethought my positions. Apparently, the price of absolution is the sacrifice of one's own moral code. So I left without redemption and it is up to me to create my penance. I wear these rags as a crown of thorns. I hate them. I have plenty of money. My father invested wisely and left me a chain of motor lodges when he died, but I've been wearing the same dress for five months now. I smell miserable, but I still feel guilty. I tried to give up television — I thought that would be sufficiently torturous to leave me feeling clean and reborn. So I threw my set into the river. But I found myself browsing, decadently, for hours, in appliance stores. I am wretchedness itself. That is why I have decided to put my eyes out with this screwdriver. Excuse me. *(She turns her back to the audience and raises the screwdriver high, over her head.)* I WILL BE CLEAN!!! *(As she stabs her eyes, her light goes out.)*

## Scene 7

*The Dixon's living room, as before. Kip is painting. Bernadette, who is now quite pregnant, is posing.*

BERNADETTE.  I think I've been pregnant for years. I can't wait to be an alcoholic.
KIP.  Finished!
BERNADETTE.  *(Sighing.)* Can I look? *(He nods and reveals the painting. It's white — on white.)* IT'S WHITE!!
KIP.  Like it? Do you? You can be honest.
BERNADETTE.  IT'S BLANK! IT'S WHITE! THERE'S NOTH-ING THERE!

KIP.   I only used white paint. I didn't want to screw up.
BERNADETTE.   You — AAAAAAAHHHHHHHHHHH! *(She clutches her middles and doubles over in pain.)* It's time! *(Blackout.)*

## Scene 8

*Sebastian's apartment, or a fragment of it. There needs to be a love seat or sofa and an end table, on which sits an open bottle of wine and two glasses. Roger is seated, reading* Vanity Fair. *Roger is meant to be played by the same actor as Dylan and, although his costume is different and he speaks with no discernible accent, there should be no effort to conceal that this is the same actor. Sebastian is pacing, nervously, watching Roger read. After a moment, Roger closes the magazine and puts it on the table.*

ROGER.   Well.
SEBASTIAN.   Well, what?
ROGER.   It was good.
SEBASTIAN.   Did you like it?
ROGER.   I did.
SEBASTIAN.   Good. Thank you.
ROGER.   I don't think I understood it.
SEBASTIAN.   What didn't you understand?
ROGER.   What it was about.
SEBASTIAN.   Oh.
ROGER.   What was it about?
SEBASTIAN.   Well, guilt and the breakdown of structure in the culture.
ROGER.   Really?
SEBASTIAN.   Yes.
ROGER.   There you are. I missed that completely.
SEBASTIAN.   *(Disappointed.)* Oh.
ROGER.   But I liked it.
SEBASTIAN.   So you think I could write about you?

ROGER. Sure.

SEBASTIAN. Good. Good. Good. I think it could be very interesting. I won't use your name if you want, if you don't want. You can decide later. I'm glad you enjoyed dinner.

ROGER. Thanks.

SEBASTIAN. So, make yourself at home. Make yourself comfortable. Relax.

ROGER. I am.

SEBASTIAN. What?

ROGER. Relaxed.

SEBASTIAN. Good.

ROGER. *(Standing.)* Where do you want to do this?

SEBASTIAN. Do what? Which?

ROGER. Whatever you want.

SEBASTIAN. That seems awfully abrupt.

ROGER. *(Sitting.)* Sorry.

SEBASTIAN. I would call that sudden. In any event, I'm not sure what I want. I mean, I know what I want in general — Did you mean the interview? Is that what you meant? Or did you mean the other.

ROGER. I meant the other.

SEBASTIAN. I see. That's what I thought. That seems sudden. I thought we could talk first. How's that? That's what I thought.

ROGER. Sure. *(Pause.)*

SEBASTIAN. I like your ... outfit

ROGER. I like your hair.

SEBASTIAN. I hate my hair. I think it's thinning.

ROGER. It's not.

SEBASTIAN. I know it's not, but I think it is. Can I ask you something?

ROGER. Sure.

SEBASTIAN. Is "Alfonzo" you're real name?

ROGER. No.

SEBASTIAN. Oh?

ROGER. It's Roger.

SEBASTIAN. I see. I was just curious. I won't use it. In the article. If you don't want me to. You can decide. You don't look like a Roger.

ROGER. No?

SEBASTIAN. I'll call you Ruth.

ROGER. Please don't. *(Pause.)*

SEBASTIAN. I am just fascinated by what you do. I think most people are.

ROGER. *(Ironic.)* Well it is very fascinating.

SEBASTIAN. What do you call it?

ROGER. What?

SEBASTIAN. What you do, for a living.

ROGER. I have dates.

SEBASTIAN. Really? That's fascinating.

ROGER. I really thought you weren't interested.

SEBASTIAN. Oh?

ROGER. You walked by so many times —

SEBASTIAN. I've never done this before.

ROGER. *(Ironic.)* Really?

SEBASTIAN. Where do you get most of your dates? Just walking by? On the street?

ROGER. Mostly in cars.

SEBASTIAN. I see.

ROGER. People drive by, they slow down. I get in.

SEBASTIAN. Aren't you frightened? It doesn't sound very safe.

ROGER. I'm careful.

SEBASTIAN. Good.

ROGER. I don't always get in. If the date looks crazy, I walk away. I got beat up once.

SEBASTIAN. What happened?

ROGER. I got beat up.

SEBASTIAN. I see. Do you have safe sex?

ROGER. Of course

SEBASTIAN. And what does it cost — to, um, well to date you?

ROGER. It depends.

SEBASTIAN. On what?

ROGER. What the date looks like.

SEBASTIAN. If he's attractive?

ROGER. If he has money.

SEBASTIAN. How can you tell?

ROGER. I guess.

SEBASTIAN. Do I look like —

ROGER. Loaded.

SEBASTIAN. You're very bad at your job. I'm sorry.

ROGER. Sometimes ten for a blow job, sometimes a hundred.

SEBASTIAN. Well, I would appreciate something mid-range — should I decide to go that route.

ROGER. Twenty-five?

SEBASTIAN. Fine. *(Roger stands and starts to unbutton his shirt.)*

ROGER. Now?

SEBASTIAN. I don't think —

ROGER. I really want you.

SEBASTIAN. *(Changing the subject.)* Do many people buy you dinner? *(Roger sits, irritated.)*

ROGER. Sometimes.

SEBASTIAN. *(Hurt.)* Oh.

ROGER. One guy buys me dinner all the time.

SEBASTIAN. Do your parents know what you do for a living?

ROGER. Of course not.

SEBASTIAN. Where are they? Where were you raised?

ROGER. Colorado. I haven't seen them in years — I figure, they figure I'm dead.

SEBASTIAN. Do you miss them?

ROGER. I don't think about it.

SEBASTIAN. Why not?

ROGER. I'd get sad and looking sad is bad for business.

SEBASTIAN. That is very beautiful. That's touching. Pithy.

ROGER. You have really nice eyes.

SEBASTIAN. How did you get started? How does someone end up —

ROGER. I haven't.

SEBASTIAN. What?

ROGER. Ended up.

SEBASTIAN. I'm sorry.

ROGER. Don't apologize.

SEBASTIAN. I'm sorry.

ROGER.   Forget it. I think you're really nice.

SEBASTIAN.   Thank you —

ROGER.   I was hoping you'd talk to me.

SEBASTIAN.   When did you start?

ROGER.   I left home when I was fifteen.

SEBASTIAN.   I left home when I was sixteen.

ROGER.   I ran away.

SEBASTIAN.   I went to Yale.

ROGER.   I joined the army.

SEBASTIAN.   What happened?

ROGER.   I got kicked out.

SEBASTIAN.   And then?

ROGER.   I came here and got a job with an escort service.

SEBASTIAN.   How was that?

ROGER.   Fine. I got fired for speed.

SEBASTIAN.   *(Excited by this.)* Are you a drug addict?! I'm not judging, I'm just asking.

ROGER.   Yes, Sebastian, I am a drug addict.

SEBASTIAN.   What kind of drugs? Anything in particular, or just drugs in general?

ROGER.   There are no general drugs addicts.

SEBASTIAN.   I must sound extremely stupid.

ROGER.   I take speed.

SEBASTIAN.   I see. *(Pause. Roger places his hand on Sebastian's thigh.)*

ROGER.   Are you ready?

SEBASTIAN.   *(Shifting, nervously.)* Have you ever been in love?

ROGER.   *(Withdrawing.)* Yes.

SEBASTIAN.   What happened?

ROGER.   Nothing.

SEBASTIAN.   Where is he now?

ROGER.   Seattle.

SEBASTIAN.   Why?

ROGER.   He's in a clinic there. He's in rehab.

SEBASTIAN.   Do you miss him?

ROGER.   Yes.

SEBASTIAN.   You love him.

ROGER.   It's good he's there. He needs to be.

SEBASTIAN.    How did you meet? *(As Roger tells his story, He seems to become quite sad, but there may be an odd flatness to it.)*
ROGER.    He worked at the service when I started and one night there was a call, this old guy wanted to watch — two of us. That's how we met.... We moved in together the next week. It was great. Benji was on his own since he was twelve. His father used to fuck him. He was a kid, so he ran away.
SEBASTIAN.    I see.
ROGER.    About a year ago, I got him to call his mother. It turns out his father died. Years ago. So anyway, when he got sick, last summer, from some bad speed — he got sick and I sent him home. I didn't know what else to do.
SEBASTIAN.    I see.
ROGER.    His mother put him where he is now. I don't know the address. I don't know the phone number. She won't tell me. *(Pause.)*
SEBASTIAN.    What does he look like?
ROGER.    He has brown hair ... like you. *(Pause.)* And dark eyes. Like you.
SEBASTIAN.    Oh.
ROGER.    And very, good lips. *(Slowly, romantically, Roger leans in and kisses Sebastian on the mouth. It is gentle at first, then becomes passionate as Sebastian responds. Then, quite suddenly, Roger grabs his wine glass, smashes it on the end table and holds it against Sebastian's throat.)* GIMMEE YOUR WALLET!
SEBASTIAN.    *(Terrified, panicked.)* What?!
ROGER.    GIMMEE YOUR FUCKING WALLET!!
SEBASTIAN.    Roger?!
ROGER.    GIVE IT TO ME, FUCKER!!
SEBASTIAN.    *(Doing so.)* Why don't you just take the money —
ROGER.    SHUT UP!!!
SEBASTIAN.    I'm just gonna stop the credit —
ROGER.    SHUT THE FUCK UP!! AND DON'T EVEN THINK ABOUT CALLING THE FUCKING COPS!! I SUCK THE COMMISSIONER'S DICK!! *(Roger runs out. Sebastian rushes to the doorway. There is blood on his throat.)*
SEBASTIAN.    ROGER!... ROGER!!... YOU DON'T HAVE

TO GO! IT'S ALL RIGHT!... LISTEN TO ME! LISTEN TO
ME, IT'S OK!... PLEASE! PLEASE COME BACK! *(Miranda
Bliss enters from the other side of the stage, or is revealed, unnoticed
by Sebastian. She carries her purse and a shower-head.)* Please come
back.... Please.

MIRANDA. What on earth is the matter with you, Sebastian?

SEBASTIAN. *(Turning around, shocked.)* What!?

MIRANDA. What is wrong with you?

SEBASTIAN. MOTHER!?

MIRANDA. *(Handing him a handkerchief.)* Here. You're
bleeding.

SEBASTIAN. *(Pressing it to his throat.)* Oh my God!

MIRANDA. How *can* you let people like that into your home?

SEBASTIAN. MY THROAT IS BLEEDING!

MIRANDA. You'll be fine.

SEBASTIAN. My neck! My God! Look!

MIRANDA. It's nothing. Try getting hit in the head with one
of these. *(She offers the shower-head for consideration.)*

SEBASTIAN. I don't understand! Am I dreaming?!

MIRANDA. You seem wide awake to me.

SEBASTIAN. Jesus God, I must be dying! I don't want to die!

MIRANDA. Please don't dramatize. It's a tiny wound, really.

SEBASTIAN. I don't understand! What's going on?

MIRANDA. You have just had your throat cut. The mystery
is nil. You have prostitutes and drug addicts in your home and
end up bleeding from the neck. Should things have come to
any other end, I would be shocked. Keep that against your
throat and sit down.

SEBASTIAN. It's not stopping!

MIRANDA. I'm so disappointed, Sebastian. What was the
purpose of this? Bringing *"this"* into your home?

SEBASTIAN. What are you talking about?

MIRANDA. And *chatting* with him. My God! Really, whores
are for sex, not conversation.

SEBASTIAN. YOU ARE DEAD!

MIRANDA. *(With great authority.)* SIT. DOWN. *(He obeys.)*

SEBASTIAN. But —

MIRANDA. I'm dead. I'm dead. Fine. You're Johnny one

note. Let's move passed that, shall we?

SEBASTIAN.   But you're here!

MIRANDA.   And I am sickened by what I see, saddened. What on earth has become of you? Are you so remote and needy that you court the affections of prostitutes?

SEBASTIAN.   I liked him.

MIRANDA.   Oh please.

SEBASTIAN.   I'm lonely.

MIRANDA.   Everyone's lonely. So what? That's no excuse for poor judgment. It's no reason to dabble in friendships with people who are so obviously, simply bad. You're on a course that can only —

SEBASTIAN.   He wasn't "bad." He was in —

MIRANDA.   He cut your throat. I'd call that bad.

SEBASTIAN.   He's desperate. He's confused. He's had a hard life.

MIRANDA.   You seem to be functioning under some idiotic, modern idea that there are no evil people in the world. It's a new-fangled and nitwit conceit. Of course there are evil people. The streets are full of them, teaming. They multiply geometrically and crowd out the rest of us.

SEBASTIAN.   What do you want from me!!

MIRANDA.   I want answers. I couldn't sleep. I want to know why you left me.

SEBASTIAN.   What?

MIRANDA.   Why did you leave?

SEBASTIAN.   We weren't married. I was your child. I grew up and left. It's the natural order.

MIRANDA.   Not the way you did it. You cut me dead. Why?

SEBASTIAN.   We spoke on the phone.

MIRANDA.   Christmas and birthdays, to remind me you were gone. Do you think I didn't need you?

SEBASTIAN.   You're not supposed to need me. I'm the child. I'm supposed to need you.

MIRANDA.   You think you didn't?

SEBASTIAN.   No. I needed to get away. I couldn't please you and I couldn't keep trying. I don't want to make you proud.

MIRANDA.   But you do. I read that piece in *Vanity Fair*. I was very proud, although I didn't understand it.

SEBASTIAN.  It was not that oblique!

MIRANDA.  It was solipsistic and pretentious.

SEBASTIAN.  It was not!

MIRANDA.  You ran away, like someone afraid of something.

SEBASTIAN.  There are things I don't remember, blank spots. I'm afraid of the blank spots. What happened? Did something happen?

MIRANDA.  Nothing *happened.*

SEBASTIAN.  Did you hit me?

MIRANDA.  Are you accusing me of something?

SEBASTIAN.  I'm asking you!

MIRANDA.  Don't raise your voice to me. I may be dead, but I'm still your mother.

SEBASTIAN.  *(Quieter.)* I'm asking you.

MIRANDA.  My God. Of course not. I never hit you and the question insults me.

SEBASTIAN.  Did you touch me? Some other way?

MIRANDA.  I did not come all this way to suffer the slings and arrows of baseless accusations.

SEBASTIAN.  Something happened!

MIRANDA.  Nothing ever happened to you. Nothing bad. There was just, something between us from the beginning.

SEBASTIAN.  I tried. You were so hard. You never said anything. I asked questions and got told to sit up straight.

MIRANDA.  The answers were humiliating.

SEBASTIAN.  How did my father die?

MIRANDA.  *(Cruel.)* He didn't.

SEBASTIAN.  What?

MIRANDA.  He never died. He's still alive.

SEBASTIAN.  I don't believe you!

MIRANDA.  He's somewhere.

SEBASTIAN.  You lied all those years!?

MIRANDA.  I don't know where.

SEBASTIAN.  You had no right!

MIRANDA.  I did what I thought was best. If I made mistakes, I made them. I'd do the same thing again.

SEBASTIAN.  Who is he?!

47

MIRANDA.    Does it really matter at this point?

SEBASTIAN.    Yes!

MIRANDA.    The past is an old movie from your childhood. Forget it.

SEBASTIAN.    Why did he leave you? Did you leave him? Did he know me? Why did it end?!

MIRANDA.    You're better not knowing!

SEBASTIAN.    I'll decide!!

MIRANDA.    I was raped!!

SEBASTIAN.    *(Stunned.)* Oh my God.

MIRANDA.    *(After a moment.)* I was raped. I was walking home from work. I was very young and very stupid. I worked then, at the Chicago Tribune, selling advertising space. I was alone. It was dark and I was walking through a parking lot. It was winter and cold. There was a man there, but I didn't see him. He stepped towards me and asked if I had a light. He had a cigarette in his hand. He looked normal. He looked ... like you. And he raped me. He grabbed my wrist and pulled me toward him and forced me down, onto the concrete and he hit my face and mumbled obscenities under his breath, falling onto my mouth. He dug his fingers into my neck. He made me perform oral sex and then he raped me and left me lying on the broken glass.

SEBASTIAN.    *(Processing this.)* I am the product ... of that.

MIRANDA.    Yes.

SEBASTIAN.    I am the child of that.

MIRANDA.    So I know that there are evil people in the world.

SEBASTIAN.    I can't ...

MIRANDA.    I know first hand. I never told my father. I was very ashamed. I left Chicago and got a tiny wooden apartment with an iron bed. After you and your sister were born I worked, hard. I sold real estate and I was good at it. At night, I cried and cried. I thought I'd never stop. And then one night — you were five, or six — you were sleeping. It was very late. And I picked you up and held you in my arms because I loved you. And I squeezed you until I thought you'd die, because I hated you. I decided that night. I decided to stop. I made the conscious decision to simply stop feeling. I loved you enough to learn to feel nothing.

SEBASTIAN.   I remember that.

MIRANDA.   You couldn't possibly.

SEBASTIAN.   I do. I think I do.

MIRANDA.   My life was not particularly pleasant. It's not particularly pleasant to never feel anything, for anyone.

SEBASTIAN.   Yes. I know.

MIRANDA.   Have you never loved anyone? I don't know you at all.

SEBASTIAN.   I did. I think. I did. It was a long time ago.

MIRANDA.   Who?

SEBASTIAN.   You would not have liked him. He was not someone of whom you would have approved. Simon.

MIRANDA.   Don't make assumptions.

SEBASTIAN.   You would've hated him.

MIRANDA.   Where is he?

SEBASTIAN.   He died.

MIRANDA.   I see.

SEBASTIAN.   Years ago.

MIRANDA.   You never told me.

SEBASTIAN.   You never asked.

MIRANDA.   I'm sorry.

SEBASTIAN.   It no longer matters.

MIRANDA.   I could have helped you. How did he die?

SEBASTIAN.   It was GRID in the beginning. AIDS at the end.

MIRANDA.   Was it very hard for you?

SEBASTIAN.   Yes it was.

MIRANDA.   Let me help now. *(Dylan appears in a pool of light on the other side of the stage. He addresses no one in particular. He looks forward as he speaks.)*

SEBASTIAN.   I was nineteen. He was twenty-three. And you couldn't get an orderly to empty the trash.

DYLAN.   Dear Sebastian,

SEBASTIAN.   The clichés of how hideous that death is are all understatement. He was a human skeleton, with fluid, secretions from an infected gland, traveling through his body.

DYLAN.   What you really want to know, what you can't ask is, did I do it? What was it like?

SEBASTIAN.   One day his leg was swollen, the next his scrotum was the size of a melon.

DYLAN.   What does it feel like —

SEBASTIAN.   He was unable to see. Insane from the cancer —

DYLAN.   To take a human life?

SEBASTIAN.   And the morphine.

DYLAN.   I went into the house. The back door was open. It was dark, but I had a flashlight and I went up the stairs.

SEBASTIAN.   No nurse would clean him when he soiled himself, so I did. And he wasn't Simon. He was no one.

DYLAN.   I went into the bedroom and he was lying on the bed, just a body, sound asleep in the dark.

SEBASTIAN.   He was just a human being.

DYLAN.   I had a baseball bat. And a knife.

SEBASTIAN.   At five in the morning, the nurse went on her break.

DYLAN.   It was the middle of the night.

SEBASTIAN.   I asked her not to, because his breathing was so shallow and I was afraid he would die —

DYLAN.   The only sound was his breathing, and my breathing.

SEBASTIAN.   And I wouldn't know it.

DYLAN.   And I didn't think about a thing.

SEBASTIAN.   So someone came to sit with me. But the nurse returned and Simon was still alive.

DYLAN.   And I hit him.

SEBASTIAN.   Then he stopped breathing.

DYLAN.   Again and again. And again.

SEBASTIAN.   And I knew it at once.

DYLAN.   What does it feel like to crush a human head? It's hard. Like breaking ice.

SEBASTIAN.   I thought I was ready.

DYLAN.   But the knife goes in easy. And blood is everywhere.

SEBASTIAN.   But I cried copious and bitter tears. And then I tried to shut his eyes, but they wouldn't close.

DYLAN.   Really, if you ask me what it feels like …

SEBASTIAN.   So I called his parents and told them that their son was dead.

DYLAN.   It feels like nothing.

SEBASTIAN.   I was his lover.

DYLAN.   Blank.

SEBASTIAN.   He died. And I didn't.

DYLAN.   They're gonna turn off the lights soon.

SEBASTIAN.   There's no reason I can think of.

MIRANDA.   You're lucky to have loved at all. *(Bernadette appears in a another pool of light. She is no longer pregnant, but holds her new baby.)*

DYLAN.   So I better sign off.

SEBASTIAN.   I'm so tired.

MIRANDA.   It's the blood. You've lost a lot of blood.

DYLAN.   Sincerely, Dylan Taylor Sinclaire.

BERNADETTE.   *(To her baby.)* You're so beautiful.

SEBASTIAN.   I can't keep ...

MIRANDA.   Lie down. *(He does so.)*

BERNADETTE.   Sleep. *(All lights fade out.)*

## END ACT ONE

51

# ACT TWO

## "Forty Dollars and a New Suit"

### Scene 1

*Three months later, evening. The living room of Kip and Bernadette's home. The decor suggest upper-middle class taste. There is a sofa, chairs, a coffee table on which sits a bowl of fruit. In one corner stands an easel, surrounded by paint supplies. There is a stack of "white paintings," perhaps leaning against the sofa. There are three exits: one leads to the outside world; one to the rest of the house; one to the nursery. As the lights come up, Kip is painting. Bernadette is talking to Hillary, who now wears dark glasses, as well as bandages on her hand. Hillary is wearing the dress she wore when she put her eyes out, only now it is even more filthy and ragged than it was.*

BERNADETTE.   I can't thank you enough for coming. Did you have any trouble finding us?
HILLARY.   *(Referring to her eyes.)* Well, just what you'd expect.
BERNADETTE.   Before I begin, would you like something to drink?
HILLARY.   Perhaps a glass of warm water?
BERNADETTE.   Do your teeth hurt?
HILLARY.   No.
BERNADETTE.   Oh ... Kip, would you get Dr. MacMahon —
HILLARY.   Hillary, please.
BERNADETTE.   All right. Would you get Hillary a glass of warm water? And I'll have some Collins mix. *(Kip sighs and exits.)*
HILLARY.   Collins mix?
BERNADETTE.   Yes. Before the baby I was very unhappy and

I wanted to become an alcoholic. I thought it would be nice to have a hobby.

HILLARY. Do you still aspire to dipsomania?

BERNADETTE. Oh no. Not at all. No, no. The baby has changed everything. Do you have any children?

HILLARY. Just my patients.

BERNADETTE. I don't think that counts. Believe me. You can't imagine how the world changes. Everything goes from black to white and vice-verse. I used to worry, when I was younger, because I was completely without goals of any kind. While my girlfriends were becoming lawyers, doctors and thingamabobs, I enjoyed shopping.

HILLARY. I enjoyed shopping. Once.

BERNADETTE. Now I recognize my lack of ambition was a blessing. I'm a breeder! Everything about the baby is so cunningly tiny! The baby has the sweetest fingernails, and absolutely precious heels!

HILLARY. Small people have small things.

BERNADETTE. It's true. And it's done wonderful things for my marriage — having a baby. Kip and I are so happy now. I mean really, really, really happy. Have you ever been married?

HILLARY. Yes.

BERNADETTE. Then you know what a torture rack it can be. *(Kip enters and hands Bernadette both drinks. She places Hillary's in her hand. Kip returns to painting.)* I was just telling Hillary how happy we are since the baby.

HILLARY. To whom are you speaking?

BERNADETTE. I'm sorry. This is my husband, Kip. Say hello, Kip.

KIP. Hello.

BERNADETTE. Aren't we happy? Since the baby?

KIP. *(Painting, barely listening.)* Very, very.

HILLARY. Does the baby have a name?

BERNADETTE. Not just yet.

KIP. We call it "the baby."

BERNADETTE. We have lots of time. It's only been three months. Why rush into things? It's such a big decision — I mean you're stuck with your name your whole life.

KIP.   I think mine was a typo.

BERNADETTE.   It has to be perfect. I figure we have years.

KIP.   *(To Hillary.)* Don't you think "Minty" is a nice name?

BERNADETTE.   It's an idiot name.

KIP.   It's been in my mother's family for years.

BERNADETTE.   It should stay there.

HILLARY.   I've never heard it before.

BERNADETTE.   He's upset because I refuse to call the baby Ruth — God, I'm hungry. Have you eaten?

HILLARY.   Today?

KIP.   I don't see why we can't.

BERNADETTE.   First of all the baby's a boy. And secondly, you can't call anything Baby Ruth! My God, what are you thinking of?

KIP.   You're inflexible.

BERNADETTE.   I'm inflexible? How can you say that?

KIP.   "Sydney's" too severe.

BERNADETTE.   I've changed my entire life to accommodate your dementia!

KIP.   *(To Hillary.)* Don't you think "Sydney's" too severe?

HILLARY.   Who's he talking to?

BERNADETTE.   Who cares?

KIP.   Dr. MacMahon —

HILLARY.   *(Raising her hand.)* Present.

KIP.   Do you like the name Sydney?

HILLARY.   My father's name was Sydney.

KIP.   *(To Bernadette.)* You rejected my second choice too.

HILLARY.   Of course Mother called him Lillian.

BERNADETTE.   *(To Kip.)* You can't call a baby Hughie.

HILLARY.   We were never close.

BERNADETTE.   *(To Kip.)* It's a sick joke.

KIP.   I don't see why.

BERNADETTE.   Please *Kip*, we'll discuss it later. Where was I?

HILLARY.   I have no idea.

BERNADETTE.   Oh. Then let me thank you for coming. I didn't know what to do, or whom else to call. I must admit, though, you're not at all what I expected.

HILLARY.   What did you expect?

BERNADETTE.   I don't know. But I never expected you to be dressed so badly — Ooops! I'm sorry. Did I say something I shouldn't have? Maybe you didn't realize you're wearing rags. You are, you know. You're wearing rags.

HILLARY.   My clothes are my burden.

BERNADETTE.   Pardon?

HILLARY.   My clothes and my blindness.

BERNADETTE.   What does that mean?

HILLARY.   I've eschewed traditional penance, the political price was simply too high, in favor of my own self-mutilation.

BERNADETTE.   Oh my.

HILLARY.   I'm presently in a period of sanctification. The burden of my sins is Sisyphusian. I do what I can.

BERNADETTE.   What sins?

HILLARY.   I live. I breath. I come into rooms and leave them.

BERNADETTE.   I don't follow.

HILLARY.   I take up too much space in the world.

BERNADETTE.   You?

HILLARY.   I have no right to the food I eat while others are hungry. I used to drink Fresca all the time and then I'd cry, having enjoyed it. Who am I to find pleasure? Without a proper place in the universe, I'm just crowding someone out. *(Bernadette stands, confused and disturbed.)*

BERNADETTE.   Oh. Well.... Perhaps this was a mistake. I'm sorry you came all this way. It was very nice meeting you.

KIP.   *(A reprimand.)* Bernadette.

HILLARY.   No, no! Please. You were going to tell me about Sebastian. Is he in trouble? Is he in some kind of pain? I want to help.

BERNADETTE.   *(Considering this.)* Well. He's here.

HILLARY.   Here! Where?! Here? Sebastian?! Speak up. Don't play games.

BERNADETTE.   Not *here* in the room.

HILLARY.   Oh.

BERNADETTE.   *Here* in the house.

HILLARY.   I'm so embarrassed.

KIP.   He's been here forever.

BERNADETTE.   He's been here two months.

KIP. It seems like forever.

BERNADETTE. He's recuperating.

HILLARY. From what? Did he have a bad fall?

BERNADETTE. *(Bewildered.)* No. His throat was cut and he nearly died. He lost a great deal of blood. It was terrible.

HILLARY. Oh my God!

BERNADETTE. I don't know how it happened. He wouldn't tell them at the hospital. He won't tell me. He won't tell anyone.

HILLARY. Is he all right?

BERNADETTE. Physically, yes.

HILLARY. What do you mean?

KIP. He's nutty as a fruitcake.

BERNADETTE. Look who's talking.

HILLARY. You were saying?

KIP. Go on.

BERNADETTE. Yes. Sebastian. From the day he was admitted to the hospital, he told stories that indicate a *serious* disturbance. He insists, i. e., for instance, that he was visited by our mother. She's dead, you know.

HILLARY. I'm so sorry.

KIP. That's the least of it. That part I buy.

BERNADETTE. Kip's on a spiritual inner journey. Destination unknown.

KIP. I just recently learned to see.

HILLARY. I just recently went blind.

BERNADETTE. Go figure.

KIP. Tell her the rest.

BERNADETTE. Well, it's not just that he claims to have seen her, he claims she told him things, hideous, vile stories. Stories so awful they taste like mud in your mouth.

HILLARY. What did he say, exactly?

BERNADETTE. Impossible things. He lives in a fantasy world of glass animals.

KIP. He's batty.

BERNADETTE. He insists my mother told him that we, my brother and I, are the progeny of some *rapist.* I get shivers saying it. I get a slightly sick feeling. You see, I know for a fact that our father was a loan accountant — or was he a zoo-keeper? I can't remember right now. Kip, which was it?!

KIP. I don't know.

BERNADETTE. The point is, he lurched into this turgid dia-tribe, bandaged from ear to ear and my heart broke into twenty pieces. I love my brother and so I had him consigned to the psychiatric ward.

HILLARY. Oh my.

BERNADETTE. Have you ever seen a psychiatric ward? Do you want more water?

HILLARY. I have and no thank you.

BERNADETTE. Then you know they're nightmarish holes of bedlam. First of all, they're full of crazy people! Everyone's shuffling about, muttering to themselves. It was grim, I tell you grim! I couldn't possibly leave him there. He's my brother, I love him! Do you have any siblings?

HILLARY. I had a dog, Scraps. Dead.

BERNADETTE. Then you can't fathom the bond. And, you know, I'd be perfectly happy to have Sebastian here, with us. I mean I would be. Really. But things are happening.

KIP. *(Happy.)* We're going to Africa!

BERNADETTE. I'll get to that — We're going to Africa.

HILLARY. Oh?

BERNADETTE. We're leaving in a month. Don't ask me why.

KIP. Life begins anew thirty days from now!

BERNADETTE. I'm so worried. I cry myself to sleep at night. I can't just leave him!

KIP. He can't take care of himself.

HILLARY. What do you mean?

BERNADETTE. Well, he lives in the nursery. I mean he LIVES in there. In the nursery. Do you think he's trying to return to a state of innocence he associates with infancy?

HILLARY. All right, sure.

BERNADETTE. You see, he NEVER comes out!

HILLARY. Does he come out to eat?

BERNADETTE. Well, yes. He does. He comes out to eat. That's true.

HILLARY. Does he come out to go to the bathroom?

BERNADETTE.  Yes. He does that too. He comes out to eat and he comes out to go to the bathroom. But he doesn't really function. All he does is play with the baby.
KIP.  Constantly.
BERNADETTE.  I don't think he's a very good influence, being crazy and all. And I think the baby's exhausted. He has dark rings under his eyes. Sebastian won't leave him alone for a second. He tries to teach him things he can't possibly be ready for — he's only three months old. He plays with the baby and then there's "The other." But that's it. He doesn't even get dressed!
HILLARY.  What is "The Other?"
KIP.  He writes.
BERNADETTE.  Letters.
HILLARY.  Oh?
BERNADETTE.  Everyday. Sometimes twice a day. Three times! He leaves them on the table when no one is looking. Letters fat as phone books, page after page. Letters without end. Letters about the letters. Letters reiterating letters and letters refuting them. I had to dip into my savings for the postage. I wasn't going to mail them at first. They're all to the same person. This convict! A murderer! The letters are tomes, voluminous to the point of bursting. And some of them are quite explicit.
HILLARY.  How do you know that?
BERNADETTE.  *(Overwrought.)* I've steamed a few open. They're insane, rambling indictments of my brother's sanity, documents to the depths of his erotic perversions. I didn't want to mail them, but they're his only link to the outside world. These vile letters are all he's got!
KIP.  Calm down.
BERNADETTE.  His only friend is someone capable of killing! He never had many friends, but he had *some* and now he's reduced to this! This state: a pajama clad shut-in carrying on a written romance with someone so terribly troubled. My heart has turned to dirt! I didn't know what to do. He has no money, no home — they terminated his lease — no friends, but this! So when I found your number in his wallet

58

I assumed it was divine providence. Tell me you'll treat him!

HILLARY.  Of course.

BERNADETTE.  Thank you so much.

HILLARY.  I'll do everything I can. I'll do my best.

BERNADETTE.  I'll get him. *(Bernadette goes to the nursery door and knocks.)* Sebastian? Sebastian!

SEBASTIAN.  *(Offstage.)* Who's there?

BERNADETTE.  It's me, Bernadette.

SEBASTIAN.  *(Offstage.)* What do you want?

BERNADETTE.  Would you come out for a bit?

SEBASTIAN.  *(Offstage.)* No.

BERNADETTE.  Please?

SEBASTIAN.  *(Offstage.)* No.

BERNADETTE.  There's someone to see you.

SEBASTIAN.  *(Offstage.)* Who?

BERNADETTE.  Dr. MacMahon.

SEBASTIAN.  *(Offstage.)* She's crazy.

BERNADETTE.  She came all this way.

SEBASTIAN.  *(Offstage.)* Tell her, "get lost!"

BERNADETTE.  I can't do that.

SEBASTIAN.  *(Offstage.)* Tell her, "fuck off!"

BERNADETTE.  *(To Hillary.)* I'm sure he doesn't mean that.

SEBASTIAN.  *(Offstage.)* Yes I do.

BERNADETTE.  Sebastian, this is very embarrassing.

SEBASTIAN.  *(Offstage.)* I'm working with the baby.

BERNADETTE.  *Please* leave the baby alone! It's just a baby.

SEBASTIAN.  *(Offstage.)* He's ready to walk!

BERNADETTE.  He can't be.

SEBASTIAN.  *(Offstage.)* He is! I think.

BERNADETTE.  I'm coming in there — Excuse me. *(Bernadette exits into the nursery. There is a long pause.)*

HILLARY.  Am I alone?!!

KIP.  I'm still here.

HILLARY.  Oh. What are you doing? Are you just staring at me? Stop it right now.

KIP.  I'm painting.

HILLARY.  Oh. Are you a painter?

KIP.  I'm painting you.

HILLARY.　Please don't.

KIP.　But you're very beautiful.

HILLARY.　I'm not.

KIP.　Maybe not in the traditional sense.

HILLARY.　*(Ironic.)* Thank you.

KIP.　But beautiful, just the same.

HILLARY.　I'm so old. My skin is like wet laundry. I look used up.

KIP.　I think I've captured that.

HILLARY.　You're making me uncomfortable.

KIP.　I'm sorry. *(Pause. Kip continues painting.)* Would you like some more water?

HILLARY.　No thank you. *(Pause.)* So tell me, how long have you and Bernadette been married?

KIP.　Several years.

HILLARY.　Several?

KIP.　Eight.

HILLARY.　I see. How did you meet?

KIP.　We met in Europe. I was sort of a refugee and she was there with her mother as a graduation gift. I looked very different then.

HILLARY.　How so?

KIP.　I had long hair and I seldom bathed.

HILLARY.　Were you rebelling against something?

KIP.　Not really. I was just poor and dirty, but my parents were poor and dirty as well. My mother was a cashier at a supermarket and my father collected garbage. I mean he was a garbage collector, not a curator of some kind.

HILLARY.　Well, you've done very well for yourself.

KIP.　I made decisions! My father thought education was effeminate. But I graduated anyway. After the commencement. I rode the subway and stole the credit cards from a man sleeping next to me. Well, I was young and very stupid.

HILLARY.　Everyone's done things they're ashamed of.

KIP.　I took the cards to the airport and boarded the next plane out of there. I landed in Holland with just the clothes on my back.

HILLARY.　I've done terrible things.

KIP. I spent a few weeks panhandling, with no plan, traveling around. Then I got a job as a tour guide at The Anne Frank House.

HILLARY. I've never been.

KIP. It's depressing.

HILLARY. I would've assumed.

KIP. That's where I met Bernadette.

HILLARY. *(Ironic.)* Touching.

KIP. She brought me back here, or her mother did. And I became a dentist.

HILLARY. Do you have a practice?

KIP. I gave it up. I paint now.

HILLARY. Have you painted your wife?

KIP. I have. My first painting was of Bernadette.

HILLARY. Is it here? May I feel it?

KIP. Pardon me?

HILLARY. May I run my hands over it? *(Kip goes to her, takes her hand and leads her to the stack of "white paintings." He pulls one out and places it in her hands.)*

KIP. Here.

HILLARY. Thank you. *(She runs her hands over the canvas.)* This is very good.

KIP. Thank you.

HILLARY. But it's not your wife.

KIP. Pardon me?

HILLARY. This is a still life of a book, a candlestick and a bowl of oranges. *(He examines the canvas very closely, and looks on the back.)*

KIP. You're exactly right!!

HILLARY. *(Proud.)* Yes. I know.

KIP. I'm sorry, I gave you the wrong — *how did you know that?*

HILLARY. I can feel the brush strokes.

KIP. You're kidding me.

HILLARY. I can read them.

KIP. That's amazing!

HILLARY. The book is *Crime and Punishment.*

KIP. You're unbelievable!!!

HILLARY. It's not so hard, really. You paint very well. *(He*

*takes the "painting" and places another in her hands.)*
KIP. Here. This one is Bernadette. *(She runs her fingers over it.)*
HILLARY. I like it. She's very beautiful.
KIP. It was my first.
HILLARY. The mouth is blurry.
KIP. She wouldn't stop talking.
HILLARY. I'm sorry. *(He removes the "painting" and places another in her hands.)*
KIP. This one is a self-portrait. *(She runs her fingers over it and becomes very sad.)*
HILLARY. It feels like my husband.
KIP. Does he have bad skin?
HILLARY. I mean it feels like it looks like him.
KIP. What does he look like?
HILLARY. He's very handsome. Or at least he was. To me. He had smooth skin and high cheekbones. Pale skin, the color of meringue. Deep set, hazel eyes and a straight nose with a small bump, which I felt made him human.
KIP. You talk about him in the past tense.
HILLARY. He left me, one day without warning.
KIP. I'm sorry. *(She hands him the "painting." He puts it away.)*
HILLARY. He wore cologne that smelled of citrus. He ran away from me.
KIP. Why?
HILLARY. Why not? I try not to dwell. If I thought about all of my failures, I'd think of nothing else. I don't want to talk about Cliff.
KIP. All right. I —
HILLARY. When he left, I thought I'd die! I shut myself in my room and stuck pins in my flesh. I made my patients the children Cliff and I never had. My lovely, neurotic children. But children hate their parents. It's true. You hated yours.
KIP. They embarrassed me, but I loved them.
HILLARY. Oh admit it! You hated their guts!
KIP. I was ambivalent.
HILLARY. Then you're a freak. In this country, in this culture children turn on their parents. Maybe not everywhere, but here, burdened down as we are, stooped over, under the

62

weight of Freud, it's true. I loathe Freud.

KIP.   I saw a documentary on television about a tribe in Africa. It was fascinating. Maybe you saw it?

HILLARY.   I threw my set in the river.

KIP.   It was on public TV.

HILLARY.   Naturally.

KIP.   Why'd you throw your set in the river?

HILLARY.   It's a long story.

KIP.   Anyway, this was a very interesting program. It was all about this one particular tribe, in Africa — and the women were treated very badly, at least by our standards —

HILLARY.   Typical.

KIP.   They were just work mules and baby machines. And the children had designated roles in life from the moment of conception. One child was a hunter. One was a shaman — I think that's the right word. And I couldn't help but wonder if these people were happy. What I mean is: Did the women feel stifled, repressed and unfulfilled? Did those children harbor bitter resentments?

HILLARY.   I suspect as much. Margaret Meade did some fascinating work in Somoa —

KIP.   Or were they free? Were they spared all of our psychological bondage because they have no words for it?

HILLARY.   That's why you want to go to Africa?

KIP.   I want to see the world in its infancy.

HILLARY.   You're too late. We've ruined everything.

KIP.   I don't believe that. (Pause.)

HILLARY.   What do you look like?

KIP.   I have smooth skin, the color of meringue, and high cheekbones. I have deep-set, hazel eyes. And a straight nose. With a bump. (Bernadette enters from the nursery, flustered.)

BERNADETTE.   He won't come out! He refuses. Flatly. He says he doesn't want to talk to you.

HILLARY.   (Disappointed.) Oh.

BERNADETTE.   But he'll have to give in eventually. I know he will. He's got to come out to eat, if I don't take him any food. He's got to come out to go to the bathroom.

KIP.   Let's hope.

BERNADETTE.  He'll be out sooner or later. Promise you'll wait. Say you'll stay!

HILLARY.  Forever.

BERNADETTE.  *(Disturbed.)* Oh.

KIP.  Wonderful!

BERNADETTE.  I'm so glad.

HILLARY.  Sebastian needs me.

BERNADETTE.  You don't have to get back to anything?

HILLARY.  I'll help him.

KIP.  We're very grateful.

BERNADETTE.  We are. Truly. You can stay here.

KIP.  It'll be fun!

BERNADETTE.  You can sleep on the sofa, right here. You'll like it, it's very uncomfortable. I used to sleep on it sometimes.

KIP.  When was that?

BERNADETTE.  Lots of times.

HILLARY.  I'll be fine. I'm sure.

BERNADETTE.  I can't thank you — Kip, go get Hillary a pillow and a blanket, would you? *(Kip exits.)* I can not tell you how much this means to me. I've been very torn. Kip is my husband and I feel I should go with him. But my brother's my brother and I won't abandon Sebastian.

HILLARY.  Of course. *(Kip enters with a pillow and a blanket.)*

KIP.  Here you go!

BERNADETTE.  Thank you. Here. Here's a pillow. And this is a blanket. *(Bernadette hands Hillary the pillow and blanket.)* Now we won't bother you any more. You must be tired after your trip. It's been a long day for all of us. The bathroom and kitchen are through — well, just shriek if you need anything. Kip is a very light sleeper.

KIP.  Please.

BERNADETTE.  Make yourself completely at home. Come on, Kip, let's leave Hillary alone. She must be exhausted.

KIP.  Goodnight.

HILLARY.  Goodnight.

BERNADETTE.  Goodnight.

HILLARY.  Goodnight. *(Kip and Bernadette exit. Hillary places the pillow on the sofa, lies down and covers herself with the blanket.*

*The lights dim gradually, suggesting the passage of time. It is the middle of the night. Then, slowly, the door to the nursery opens. Sebastian, dressed in pajamas, sneaks quietly out. Carrying several letters, he crosses to the table. As he places the letters on the table, Hillary sits up with a start.)* Who's there? *(Sebastian turns to her and is startled, at first, by what he sees.)*

SEBASTIAN.   You're blind.

HILLARY.   Sebastian. I'm so happy to hear your voice. I never thought I would. I've missed you so much. I've worried about you. We can be friends now. We can begin again.

SEBASTIAN.   I have nothing to say to you.

HILLARY.   Don't say that. Please! Sebastian, try. Talk to me. So much has happened since we last spoke, so many things. I am someone else now. I am a different person. *(Sebastian tiptoes silently back to the nursery. Hillary doesn't hear this and continues talking to where he was.)* I have secrets. I didn't want to tell you this, because I feared it would shake your faith in me, as a psychologist. But the fact is, you were my last patient. My very last. The last to go. Sad, isn't it? I know what you're thinking. What about that terribly sad-looking woman who was always in the outer office as you left? That was the cleaning woman, Irene. *(Sebastian is gone. The nursery door closes.)* She wasn't neurotic, she just vacuumed. And not very well at that. I used to make sure she always got there fifteen minutes early, so you'd think she was a patient. The truth is, you were it. And after you left, I was lost. I know it was my fault. I was a wretched doctor. I didn't know the right questions and I couldn't hear the answers for my sobbing in my head. I punished myself. You see? I have no eyes. But it wasn't enough. I still felt adrift. I know now. Psychiatry is a fraud, Sebastian. I needed God. Not religion. God. There are no systems. We've ruined them. The systems are empty — Freud is the Pope in modern dress. I was lost.... Then, one Sunday, this summer, after you left, I offered myself to God. I woke up very early. I didn't plan to. I just woke up and felt the sun in my room. I went out and walked. I walked and walked, shoeless, making holes in my feet. I walked away from the sun, west to the water. I crossed the pier, which was covered with bodies, twisted and lopping over each other. I thought they were corpses. But then I accidentally stepped on a couple and realized they were just gay men sunbathing, worshipping their God. I hope I didn't offend you. I'm not making a judgment. I just assumed they were gay because when I tripped, I fell on top of a couple who were wearing very tiny Speedo swimsuits. So I assumed. I was saying, I walked past the bodies to the edge of the pier and stood there several minutes, letting the wind ruffle my hair. I became very calm. I let myself go and fell into the water. I was baptized. I had a mikvah. I was born. And now I'm ready. I am, at last prepared to help you. I will give you God and show you beauty. I will bathe you in the powerful, divine, white, erogenic light of God! I will save you! I only ever wanted that! And to love you! I only wanted to be a part of you! *(She goes to her knees, arms extended,.)* Let me love you! I am ready! Let me love you! Let me help you!! LET ME BE PART OF YOU, THE SMALLEST PART!!! LET ME LOVE YOU!!!! *(Blackout.)*

## Scene 2

*One month later, afternoon. The living room. The easel and "paintings" are gone. The sofa is not made up as a bed. Bernadette is seated, cradling a teddy bear. Kip, rushes in, excited, carrying mail.*

KIP. The mail's here!
BERNADETTE. *(In "baby voice.")* Oh. *(In natural voice:)* Oh.
KIP. *(Sorting through the mail.)* They better be here — what are you doing?
BERNADETTE. Practicing.
KIP. Practicing what?
BERNADETTE. Talking.
KIP. You talk perfectly well —
BERNADETTE. Talking to the baby.
KIP. Don't you?

66

BERNADETTE.    Sebastian says tests prove that babies respond to tiny, high-pitched, baby voices. And that I shouldn't talk to him in my natural voice. My natural voice probably gives the baby headaches.

KIP.    *(Handing her a letter.)* Something for Sebastian. *(She takes the letter, looks at it and puts it on the table.)* HERE THEY ARE!

BERNADETTE.    *(Flat.)* Oh good.

KIP.    They would wait till the last minute. Everything good comes at the end of something, or maybe things just seem to end when something good happens — it doesn't matter. THEY'RE HERE! Our passport to a brand new life! We can shed our past and be Adam and Eve. The envelope is vibrating!

BERNADETTE.    You're vibrating. You're holding the envelope.

KIP.    EVERYTHING IS EXCITING! EVERY SENTENCE ENDS IN EXCLAMATION POINTS!

BERNADETTE.    Because you're shouting.

KIP.    Sometimes in life things just snap into perspective. What was blurry becomes suddenly clear. My eyes are hungry for new details — look at this house!

BERNADETTE.    What's wrong with it?

KIP.    Everything is so mundane! Where did we get this furniture? From a catalogue? We're about to begin the adventure of our life!

BERNADETTE.    I didn't talk to him.

KIP.    I knew it.

BERNADETTE.    I meant to —

KIP.    You've been avoiding it for weeks.

BERNADETTE.    That's not altogether true.

KIP.    You're afraid to tell him.

BERNADETTE.    Why is it *my* job?

KIP.    He's *your* brother.

BERNADETTE.    We could leave him a note.

KIP.    That'd be cruel.

BERNADETTE.    We could say it with flowers?

KIP.    We've discussed it, Bernadette. We've decided. Plans have been made, bargains struck, vaccines injected and passports updated.

BERNADETTE.    *(Standing.)* I'm going to finish packing.

KIP. You haven't packed?!

BERNADETTE. I tried. But I just stand there and stand there with all my dresses laid out on the bed and coordinating accessories draped over the pillows. I study them and stare at them, and I don't know what to take! Nothing seems to match up! Every time I try, I burst into tears!

KIP. You cry entirely too easily.

BERNADETTE. I like the blue dress with the matching bolero, but it pinches and leaves red welts on my waste. I don't know if the purple one is dressy enough —

KIP. For what?

BERNADETTE. For dinner.

KIP. In the jungle?

BERNADETTE. What if someone invites us to dinner?

KIP. They won't!

BERNADETTE. They might. You don't know that. You can't tell what's going to happen. We could get invited to dinner and I'd hate to be embarrassed by my outfit. There's nothing worse than being underdressed, unless it's being over dressed.

KIP. I'll pack for you.

BERNADETTE. You don't know a thing about fashion.

KIP. I know what I like.

BERNADETTE. Look at yourself. Look at your shoes and belt combination. Do you think they go together? I guess it's a good thing you only paint white, because you're obviously color blind.

KIP. I'm going to pack for you. Now. While you talk to your brother. *(Kip exits. Bernadette kisses the teddy bear, then crosses, cautiously to the nursery. She knocks on the door. Sebastian opens it a crack. He is wearing a shirt with pajama bottoms.)*

SEBASTIAN. Yes?

BERNADETTE. Sebastian, you're wearing a shirt!

SEBASTIAN. What do you want?

BERNADETTE. It's a sign. You're on the road to recovery. You're getting better.

SEBASTIAN. Better than what?

BERNADETTE. You're out of pajamas.

SEBASTIAN. The baby spit up on me.

BERNADETTE.  Oh.

SEBASTIAN.  He's walking now.

BERNADETTE.  He can't walk.

SEBASTIAN.  He is.

BERNADETTE.  He's four months old.

SEBASTIAN.  You're extremely negative. Your low expectations are bound to be met by life.

BERNADETTE.  Don't lecture me.

SEBASTIAN.  People can do anything they put their minds to.

BERNADETTE.  Not *babies.*

SEBASTIAN.  Look for yourself! *(She looks into the nursery.)*

BERNADETTE.  He's sleeping.

SEBASTIAN.  *(Spinning around.)* What!?

BERNADETTE.  The baby is sound asleep, and thank goodness.

SEBASTIAN.  Well, he's tired. He must've walked miles so naturally, he's tired. But he was walking!

BERNADETTE.  Sleepwalking?

SEBASTIAN.  Leave me alone. Is "she" here?

BERNADETTE.  No.

SEBASTIAN.  Thank God. I'm starved. *(Sebastian rushes out of the nursery and to the fruit bowl on the table. He takes a bite from an apple.)*

BERNADETTE.  I have to talk to you, Sebastian.

SEBASTIAN.  Where is she anyway?

BERNADETTE.  I don't know. She called a taxi early this morning.

SEBASTIAN.  Is she coming back?

BERNADETTE.  Of course.

SEBASTIAN.  Damn. *(He notices the letter on the table.)* What's this?

BERNADETTE.  It came today. Please sit down and listen to me. *(He drops the apple and tears open the letter, quite excitedly. He doesn't hear her at all.)* Kip and I have made plans. This affects you, Sebastian. We're — *(The general lighting goes out abruptly, leaving Sebastian isolated in a pool of light. He reads the letter.)*

SEBASTIAN.  Dear Sebastian, I haven't written you in quite a while, several months really. Because I wasn't sure how to respond to the letters I have received. *(A second pool of light comes up on Dylan, who looks straight ahead as he speaks.)*

SEBASTIAN and DYLAN.   You have written to me so much. So often. I have nearly been crowded out of my cell by the thousands of pages you have sent.

DYLAN.   I have burned my eyes reading the millions of words you have written. I hope you do not think I didn't write because I was not sorry about what happened to you. I was. Sincerely. But I think, I find your letters have changed. And I did not know what to think. You write me that —

SEBASTIAN.   I lie on the floor at night, in the dark, by myself,

DYLAN.   In my nephew's nursery.

SEBASTIAN.   And I imagine that you are lying next to me. I imagine I can hear your breathing and feel it cool on my face.

DYLAN.   You write:

SEBASTIAN.   I can feel your skin and your arms around me.

DYLAN.   I can see you.

SEBASTIAN.   When the room is dark enough. And you look peaceful. Like a child, asleep next to me. I wish you would be peaceful. I would love you and protect you. I would take away everything that hurts you. I would have you curl up, inside of me and stay there forever.

DYLAN.   You write:

SEBASTIAN.   I run my fingers over your face and your skin is smooth. Your hair smells clean. I put my mouth on your mouth and on your neck and your cock and I taste you. You smile, groggy, because you are happy and safe. You taste salty to my tongue.

DYLAN.   *(After a moment.)* And you say:

SEBASTIAN.   I love you.

DYLAN.   In thousands of ways and hundreds of languages. *(Sebastian now looks at Dylan, who looks ahead.)*

SEBASTIAN.   I love you. *(Pause.)*

DYLAN.   *(A powerful command.)* DO NOT.

SEBASTIAN.   I love you.

DYLAN.   I look at my hands. They are just hands. They are

like your hands. But, they have taken a life.

SEBASTIAN. So?

DYLAN. You don't *want* to know so many things.

SEBASTIAN. I love you.

DYLAN. I have done horrible things! I have done things I wish I had only imagined. Things beyond my ability to believe! And I can blame forever. I can blame my parents and God, and drugs, and you, and be right every time!! — But they are my hands. I own them. They do what I tell them.

SEBASTIAN. I love you!

DYLAN. When I came here, it was like a dream. I have watched myself for a very long time. I have *hated me for years.* I lie, awake, at night and I am sick, truly sick, with poison in my bowels because I am *me.* I am dying, knowing there is something wrong in *me.* Something missing in *me*!!

SEBASTIAN. Me!

DYLAN. I have thought I am not human when I wanted to cry and found I could not. And who will feel pity for me?! I have what I earned.

SEBASTIAN. No!

DYLAN. I have wanted to die and tried to! But whatever I am, I am incapable or unwilling to accomplish that. And no one will help me! I am trapped in the person of myself!!

SEBASTIAN. I love you!

DYLAN. I WANT IT TO STOP! The only thing I feel is a terrible, black, sick, hate! I have been punished and punished myself! And it does not work! It does not stop! I want to cut off my hands! I cannot undo what they have done! BUT I CAN DO SOMETHING ELSE!

SEBASTIAN. Don't!

DYLAN. Do not write me anymore, Sebastian. I am killing you.

SEBASTIAN. NO!

DYLAN. You have written me too much! You're a sad, lonely human being!

SEBASTIAN. NO!

DYLAN. I AM KILLING YOU!

SEBASTIAN. NO!

DYLAN.   You have *nothing else* and see *nothing else* and want *nothing else,* because I am everything and it is KILLING YOU. I AM KILLING YOU! AND I WILL NOT DO THIS AGAIN!

SEBASTIAN.   PLEASE NO!!!!

DYLAN.   *(Still.)* You have been kind to me and you will think I am cruel, but I am trying to save you ...

SEBASTIAN.   ... no.

DYLAN.   Do not write me again. I will not open your letters. And I will never respond. *(Pause. Dylan looks at Sebastian.)* I release you. *(Dylan leaves his pool of light and crosses to Sebastian. They look at each other for a moment, very close. Then they kiss. After a moment, Dylan breaks the embrace. He turns and exits, slowly, leaving Sebastian alone in his pool of light. Sebastian is shattered and slowly turns his back to the audience. The general lighting returns, abruptly. Kip and Hillary have joined Sebastian and Bernadette in the room. Kip is standing at one end, with suitcases. Hillary is standing in the doorway. Her arms are extended and party hats hang from her wrists.)*

HILLARY.   Bon Voyage!

KIP.   How wonderful!

HILLARY.   I couldn't let you leave without a proper send off!

KIP.   That's extremely generous of you, Hillary. Isn't that sweet of Hillary?

BERNADETTE.   You packed?

KIP.   Two pairs of pants and plenty of tee shirts. You'll fit in anywhere.

BERNADETTE.   I hope not.

HILLARY.   Bon Voyage! Good Voyage! *(Kip takes the hats from Hillary. He puts one on, and proceeds to put hats on Hillary, Bernadette and Sebastian.)*

KIP.   Isn't this exciting? This is festive.

BERNADETTE.   The hats say happy birthday.

HILLARY.   Do they? I'm so sorry.

KIP.   It doesn't matter. *(To Bernadette.)* You look beautiful!

HILLARY.   I tried to make a cake last night. I stayed up all night long. But I kept burning my fingers.

KIP.   The effort was sweet.

HILLARY.   I wouldn't've been able to write on the cake anyway.

KIP.   *(Putting a hat on Sebastian.)* It's the thought that counts.

HILLARY.   I did get noisemakers!

KIP.   I love noisemakers!

BERNADETTE.   *(Hillary blows a noisemaker.)* You'll wake the baby.

HILLARY.   Sorry.

KIP.   They always remind me of New Year's Eve when everything is full of hope for fresh beginnings, a chance to redesign yourself!

BERNADETTE.   New Year's Eve makes me nervous. No matter where I go, I'm dressed inappropriately. I wear something simple, everyone's in black tie and vice-verse.

HILLARY.   I'm very sorry the hats say "happy birthday." The man at the store told me they said "bon voyage." I can't read glitter.

BERNADETTE.   I always get indigestion on New Year's Eve.

HILLARY.   I think he hated me. He had terrible body odor and I'm hyper sensitive to that kind of thing lately.

KIP.   It doesn't matter one bit and I won't tolerate your feeling bad about it. In a way, this is our birthday. We've been in utero for years. But tonight we'll soar, like Pegasus, across the sky, among the stars and be finally born!

BERNADETTE.   *(Tugging her hat.)* The elastic hurts my neck.

HILLARY.   I feel sad. I'm sorry, but I can't help it. The house will seem so empty without you.

KIP.   We'll miss you too.

BERNADETTE.   *(Removing her hat.)* I can't breath. I'm not wearing this.

KIP.   We'll write you postcards every fifteen minutes.

HILLARY.   Please don't. I couldn't read them anyway.

KIP.   We'll write in Braille. *(Sebastian finally turns around.)*

SEBASTIAN.   What's going on?

HILLARY.   Sebastian! You're out!?

SEBASTIAN.   What's going on here?

KIP.   *(To Bernadette.)* Did you tell him?

BERNADETTE.   I couldn't.

HILLARY.     Sebastian, I'm so glad you're out. *(Hillary walks towards Sebastian, who dashes away from her.)*

KIP.     What do you mean you couldn't?

HILLARY.     Where are you?

BERNADETTE.     I tried to, but —

SEBASTIAN.     Tell me what? What does everyone know but me?

KIP.     Tell him.

SEBASTIAN.     What kind of plot's been hatched? What is everyone talking about? And why am I wearing this idiotic hat!? *(Sebastian throws his hat on the floor.)*

BERNADETTE.     It's nothing —

KIP.     We're going away. *(Hillary blows her noisemaker.)*

BERNADETTE.     Please don't do that!

HILLARY.     Sorry.

SEBASTIAN.     What do you mean "going away?" Going where?

BERNADETTE.     Kip and I are going to Africa.

KIP.     You should've told him before now.

SEBASTIAN.     Africa? What are you talking about? For how long?!

KIP.     Forever.

BERNADETTE.     To live.

KIP.     Your sister and I are going to live in Africa.

SEBASTIAN.     When?! When are you going?

KIP.     Tonight.

BERNADETTE.     In a little while.

SEBASTIAN.     Why on earth?

KIP.     Human beings and plants, the earth unspoiled!! We can lose our neurosis and fears. We'll shed our psychology with our clothes in Africa!! It's New Year's Eve and we can remake ourselves — drunk on beauty that burns the eyes!!

SEBASTIAN.     Are you having a seizure of some kind?!!

KIP.     We're going to die, Sebastian. We're all going to die — at least I am — and I will not spend what's left in regret. Opportunities are all around us! We're just too blind to see — sorry.

HILLARY.     Forget it.

SEBASTIAN.     Are you sick?

KIP.     I'm fine thanks.

SEBASTIAN.   What do you mean, you're going to die?

KIP.   Well, someday —

SEBASTIAN.   SOMEDAY! Big news! Your life has a beginning, a middle and end.

KIP.   I have only beginnings now.

HILLARY.   That's beautiful. You should write for Hallmark. You speak in verse.

SEBASTIAN.   *(To Bernadette.)* Do you want this? Do you want to go?

BERNADETTE.   I don't know! I want to be an alcoholic again!

KIP.   Again?!

BERNADETTE.   I mean I *want* it again!

SEBASTIAN.   This is very upsetting. I'm going to be sick.

KIP.   *(To Hillary.)* Can you write a prescription?

HILLARY.   *(Shaking her head.)* I'm a psychologist.

SEBASTIAN.   What about the baby?

BERNADETTE.   We're taking the baby.

KIP.   Of course.

SEBASTIAN.   *(Exploding.)* You can't! YOU JUST CAN'T!

KIP.   We can do anything we want!

BERNADETTE.   I'm sorry!

KIP.   It's our baby.

SEBASTIAN.   I love him!!!

BERNADETTE.   Oh God.

KIP.   When you're better you can come and visit.

SEBASTIAN.   I'm fine now! There's nothing wrong with me! I know what this is. This is some kind of plot. I hear you gossiping and scheming. "He doesn't come out. He never leaves the nursery." Why should I? I love the baby and I don't like you!!

KIP.   Well!

SEBASTIAN.   "He doesn't get dressed. He lives in pajamas." Tell me. Where am I going that I should get dressed?!!

BERNADETTE.   I knew there'd be a scene!

SEBASTIAN.   YOU CANNOT TAKE THE BABY! He's special! He needs special attention! He has gifts you don't understand. He's BRILLIANT!!

KIP.   He's four months old!

SEBASTIAN. *(Quite bitter.)* And he's more intelligent right now than you'll ever be! He loves me. I play with him and teach him things. He stares at me with no judgment, or fear, or anything. He looks at me like sad dogs playing poker. Total acceptance. You don't even know him. Did you know that he walked today?

KIP. That's impossible.

SEBASTIAN. Of course you didn't!! You were on some "inner journey." Your psychic pretensions are pathological. Your gestalts are greed in sheep's clothing!!

KIP. You hallucinate!!

SEBASTIAN. And what's supposed to happen to me? Do I get carted off, back to the loony bin? Why am I being punished?!!

HILLARY. *(To the heavens.)* Why is anyone?!!

SEBASTIAN. *(To Bernadette.)* I'm not crazy. You're the crazy one. Weeping all the time like a broken doll, vomiting after every meal.

BERNADETTE. I gave that up.

SEBASTIAN. Next to you, I'm sanity's poster boy. You, with all your nerve endings swollen and exposed, dragging an innocent baby off to Africa, where it simply cannot be safe!

KIP. Tell it to the Africans!

SEBASTIAN. When I get to the mental ward, I'm going straight to leather shop and make a gun and kill myself.

BERNADETTE. No one is sending you anywhere. You can stay here.

HILLARY. With me!

SEBASTIAN. Is this April fools?!!

HILLARY. I'm going to stay and work with you.

SEBASTIAN. *(Flat.)* I hate her.

HILLARY. Give me another chance! That's all I ask! I've eschewed the traditional science of the mind! Take my hand and walk with me to God!! *(Hillary is groping for Sebastian, chasing him, staggering blindly.)*

SEBASTIAN. You're crazy!

HILLARY. Doctors are lucky. Parents never get another chance. They slash their children with knives and the wounds never heal. Doctors get to try again and again.

SEBASTIAN.  I'd cut out my tongue rather than tell you the time!

HILLARY.  Be my eyes. I'll be your soul.

SEBASTIAN.  How can you leave me with her?!

BERNADETTE.  She means well.

SEBASTIAN.  She does not. She's evil! She's been sleeping with Kip!!!

KIP.  What?!

SEBASTIAN.  Didn't you know that? He comes out in the middle of the night and they make love right here. It's true!

KIP.  It's not!

SEBASTIAN.  Hot, sweaty, clandestine sex, in the missionary position, on this sofa, in your house!

KIP.  Can there be a point to these masturbatory fantasies?

SEBASTIAN.  They fuck in your living room! And now you want to make the room and ME a gift to HER?

KIP.  I don't think Hillary can help you. You're beyond repair!!

HILLARY.  It's true! WE DID! WE HAVE! WE DID!

KIP.  Hillary!?

HILLARY.  Make a clean breast of things! It's better, Kip!!

KIP.  I don't know what she's talking about.

HILLARY.  I can live with it no longer!!

KIP.  *(To Hillary.)* Be quiet!

HILLARY.  I sinned! I was weak! I am weak! What can I expect of me? I have always been so bad! When I was a little girl my parents were mean to me, so I was mean to Scraps — I burned his skin with cigarettes. *I want to die!!*

SEBASTIAN.  This is who's to take care of me?

HILLARY.  I feel better having admitted things, *but dirty having done them.*

SEBASTIAN.  Well, of course you do. You *never* bathe.

HILLARY.  I have to be punished.

KIP.  *(To Bernadette.)* Don't believe her. She's lying, or confused. Maybe it was Sebastian. She's blind. She could be wrong.

HILLARY.  *(To Sebastian.)* Will you punish me?

KIP. *(To Bernadette.)* Let's go now.

SEBASTIAN. *(To Hillary.)* Gladly.

KIP. Let's just leave them. We'll watch the planes take off, carrying all kinds of people to all kinds of places. Flight 708 leaving now for tomorrow. Flight 801 boarding for new beginnings.

HILLARY. *(On her knees.)* Bernadette, I'm sorry. Believe me. I am. I never meant to hurt you. I never meant to hurt anyone.

BERNADETTE. Apology accepted.

SEBASTIAN. WHAT!?

BERNADETTE. So they had an affair. So what? What am I supposed to do? Fly into rage? Burst into tears? Why?!

HILLARY. I can't help what I feel for Kip.

BERNADETTE. What do you feel?

HILLARY. I hate him for leaving me.

KIP. *(To Bernadette.)* Flight 905 boarding now for forgotten pasts!

HILLARY. *(To the heavens.)* Everyone leaves me!

SEBASTIAN. Dear God! Not that song and dance.

HILLARY. My mother put teddy bears in my line of vision and out of my reach. I should never've been born.

KIP. Can we please go now, Bernadette?

BERNADETTE. Quiet. I'm listening to Hillary.

HILLARY. *(Standing.)* I'm sorry Kip. I am. You can hate me if you want, but I can't help it — I tried to adopt a brave front and pretend I was thrilled — I bought hats! —

KIP. *(To Bernadette.)* Flight 101 away from lunatics.

HILLARY. It's not your fault, Kip. You never misled me. You never made promises, or swore oaths or whispered you loved me while lying on top of me. I thought I could be strong, BUT I CAN'T!! You held me in your arms and I thought I'd explode!! How am I supposed to let you walk away? What am I left with but Sebastian, who loathes me with a bottomless venom?

SEBASTIAN. You got that right.

HILLARY. I CAN FIND NO PEACE!!! I've tortured myself like the Spanish Inquisition and still I'm mired in the muck of self-hate! I refuse to continue ... YOU WILL NOT LEAVE

ME, KIP! I can't survive it. I'll leave! I'LL LEAVE YOU! I'LL GO FIRST! Let me walk away, do me that favor — I'm sorry, Sebastian, I wanted to help you, but I can't do it, and I won't do it at my own expense. Good-bye. *(Hillary exits. Sebastian goes to the nursery and stands in the doorway.)*

KIP.    Believe me, Bernadette, it was nothing. It meant less than nothing.

BERNADETTE.    Don't speak!

KIP.    She blew everything out of proportion.

BERNADETTE.    *(Powerful.)* Go after her.

KIP.    What?

BERNADETTE.    Go. Get her.

KIP.    I love you.

BERNADETTE.    I doubt that. I doubt it very much.

KIP.    We'll put this behind us.

BERNADETTE.    *(Calm, without rancor.)* In any event, I don't love you.

KIP.    I don't understand.

BERNADETTE.    A simpler sentence has seldom been uttered.

KIP.    What are you saying?

BERNADETTE.    Can't we be honest, at last, for once? How long can we possibly pretend we're happy? A year? Many years? The rest of our lives, I suppose. But one more day will break me.... Go after her. We're strangers, really. You see a world in dreams and I don't want to. I have to find some happiness in things, things I can touch, my things, my child, my skin. So go.

KIP.    You're angry with me.

BERNADETTE.    No. You rescued me. I'm aware of that. And I, you.

KIP.    I don't know what you're talking about.

BERNADETTE.    I was a prisoner in my mother's life and I was miserable. I was raised under water and I couldn't breath. I needed an escape and you provided.

KIP.    Flight 707 leaving for tonight —

BERNADETTE.    I no longer need you. We've made so many compromises and told so many lies. I thought I only deserved crumbs — Don't worry, Kip. You'll have money. I'll see to that.

You helped me escape, and more than that, you gave me what I wanted when I didn't know I wanted it. A child, the chance to do something right. But don't insult me with *feelings*. I think, I always knew, you didn't love me either. You simply hated your life as much as I hated mine. So can't we call things even and go our separate ways? You'll never be poor. I owe you everything. Here. *(She holds out the tickets to Kip.)*

KIP. *(After a moment.)* What about the baby?

BERNADETTE. He'll be fine.

KIP. He needs a father.

SEBASTIAN. I'll be the father.

KIP. You?

SEBASTIAN. I love him.

BERNADETTE. Did you ever really want the baby? Do you want the baby?

KIP. Yes.

BERNADETTE. Do you hold him? *(No response.)* Do you let him know? *(No response.)*

SEBASTIAN. I'll be the father. I'll do a good job. I'll do my best.

BERNADETTE. Here. Take Hillary.

KIP. I don't know where she went. *(Bernadette goes to the door and looks out.)*

BERNADETTE. She's a blind woman. She's standing on the lawn. *(Kip goes to the nursery and looks in for a moment. Then he picks up the luggage and approaches Bernadette.)*

KIP. Thank you.

BERNADETTE. Thank you. *(He takes the tickets and kisses her good-bye. It is not passionate, but, rather, loving and gentle. He exits. Bernadette closes the door behind him.)*

SEBASTIAN. Are you all right? *(Bernadette nods.)* Upset? *(Bernadette shakes her head "no.")* Sad?

BERNADETTE. I feel like taking off my clothes and singing.

SEBASTIAN. Please don't. *(He looks into the nursery.)* Bernadette! Come here! Come here quickly! *(She goes to the nursery door.)*

BERNADETTE. What is it?

SEBASTIAN. He's walking.

BERNADETTE. My God.

SEBASTIAN. I told you.

BERNADETTE. He's walking. *(Sebastian leaves the nursery door and picks up his discarded party hat.)*

SEBASTIAN. He's brilliant.

BERNADETTE. It's a miracle.

SEBASTIAN. Bernadette?

BERNADETTE. He's lying down.

SEBASTIAN. Can I ask you something?

BERNADETTE. What?

SEBASTIAN. Can we call him, Simon?

BERNADETTE. *(Turning to him.)* Simon?

SEBASTIAN. I'd like to name the baby Simon.

BERNADETTE. Who's Simon?

SEBASTIAN. Someone I loved.

BERNADETTE. Oh.

SEBASTIAN. Who died.

BERNADETTE. I'm sorry.

SEBASTIAN. I held his hand and helped him. And I really cared for him. He was very smart. And very beautiful. To me.

BERNADETTE. He sounds very nice.

SEBASTIAN. He wasn't. Really. Before he died, he slept with several people. I think. Willfully.

BERNADETTE. Oh?

SEBASTIAN. I think he killed them. *(He turns away from her.)*

BERNADETTE. Oh.

SEBASTIAN. I never said that before. I think he did. I think he meant to. *(He starts to cry.)* But I loved ... *(Inaudible:)* him.

BERNADETTE. Well ... people —

SEBASTIAN. I miss him.

BERNADETTE. Are you crying?

SEBASTIAN. *(Hiding.)* I miss him. *(She goes to him and holds him.)*

BERNADETTE. Good.

SEBASTIAN. I miss him.

BERNADETTE. Cry.

SEBASTIAN. I miss everyone.

BERNADETTE. I know.

SEBASTIAN.   I do.
BERNADETTE.   Ssshh. Everything is fine.
SEBASTIAN.   I miss mother.
BERNADETTE.   Everything is wonderful. *(She comforts him. Fade-out.)*

**END OF PLAY**

# PROPERTY LIST

Book *(Helter Skelter)*
Desk, wheels unlocked, with:
      pad
      pen
      pencil (with pens and pencil)
      Kleenex box
      letter opener
      blotter
Chair
Letter and envelope (from Dylan)
Stool
Screwdriver
Bandages
Purse
Handkerchief (rigged with blood)
Shower head
Letter, unsealed (from Dylan)
Mail
      letter to Sebastian in envelope
      airline tickets
      catalogue
Party hats
Noisemakers
Wallet with money
2 wine glasses
Bottle of wine, open
Easel with canvas
Paint table with:
      brushes
      paint supplies
Bowl of fruit, with apple
Switch blade
Baby

Glass of water
Glass of Collins mix
Pillow
Blanket
Teddy bear
2 suitcases
White paintings
Letters, sealed (to Dylan)

# COSTUME PLOT

**ACT ONE, Scene 1:**
Blue blazer
Blue chambray shirt
T-shirt
Tie (navy knit)
Belt
Trousers (olive)
Socks
Shoes (Doc Martins)

**ACT ONE, Scene 2:**
Repeat everything

**ACT ONE, Scene 4:**
Brown striped shirt
Repeat T-shirt
Repeat pants and belt
Repeat shoes and socks

**ACT ONE, Scene 6:**
Repeat Scene 4

**ACT ONE, Scene 8:**
Burgundy shirt
Repeat pants and belt
Repeat shoes and socks

**ACT TWO, Scene 1:**
Pajamas top and bottom
White socks
T-shirt

**ACT TWO, Scene 2:**
>Dress shirt
>Repeat pajamas bottom and socks

## BERNADETTE DIXON

**ACT ONE, Scene 1:**
>Black dress
>Black opaque tights
>Gold heart locket
>Black shoes

**ACT ONE, Scene 3:**
>Pale pink nightgown

**ACT ONE, Scene 4:**
>Repeat nightgown
>Blue robe
>Slippers

**ACT ONE, Scene 5:**
>Burgundy evening gown
>Stockings
>Taupe shoes

**ACT ONE, Scene 6:**
>Repeat Scene 5
>Add four-month pregnancy pad

**ACT ONE, Scene 7:**
>Repeat Scene 5
>Add nine-month pregnancy pad

**ACT ONE, Scene 8:**
>Peach nightgown-robe set
>Slippers

**ACT TWO, Scene 1:**
> Red silk knit top
> Tan skirt
> Taupe shoes
> Taupe stockings
> Repeat locket

**ACT TWO, Scene 2:**
> Ecru lace stretch top
> Navy wrap skirt (mid-calf)
> Repeat stockings
> Navy shoes

## KIP DIXON

**ACT ONE, Scene 1:**
> Navy suit
> White shirt
> Navy tie
> Socks
> Black belt
> Black wing-tip shoes

**ACT ONE, Scene 3:**
> Striped pajamas
> Slippers

**ACT ONE, Scene 5:**
> Paint smock
> Shirt
> Khaki pants
> Socks
> Topsider shoes

**ACT ONE, Scene 6:**
> Green shirt
> Repeat pants, shoes, socks

**ACT ONE, Scene 7:**
>Paint smock (with white paint)
>Repeat Scene 6

**ACT TWO, Scene 1:**
>Blue shirt
>Repeat Scene 6

**ACT TWO, Scene 2:**
>Safari hat
>Safari jacket
>Dark safari shirt
>Ivory safari pants
>Tan belt
>Tan socks
>Repeat black shoes


## HILLARY MACMAHON
**ACT ONE, Scene 1:**
>Check jacket
>Purple dress #1
>Black belt
>Pocket square
>Reading glasses
>Black lace boots
>Miscellaneous jewelry

**ACT ONE, Scene 6:**
>Purple dress #2 (distressed)
>Distressed stockings
>Black lace boots # 2 (distressed)

**ACT TWO, Scene 1:**
>Purple dress #3 (very distressed)
>Dark glasses
>Repeat boots and stockings

**ACT TWO, Scene 2:**
> Repeat Act One, Scene 1

## MIRANDA

**ACT ONE, Scene 8:**
> Wig
> Pearl earrings
> Pearl necklace
> Taupe dress/jacket set (period)
> Taupe stockings
> Taupe shoes
> Purse
> Gloves

## DYLAN

**All Scenes:**
> Eyeglasses (round gold rimmed)
> White T-shirt
> Orange coveralls
> Socks
> White sneakers

## ROGER

> Bandanna (worn on head)
> Plaid shirt with hood
> Black jeans
> Black high-top sneakers

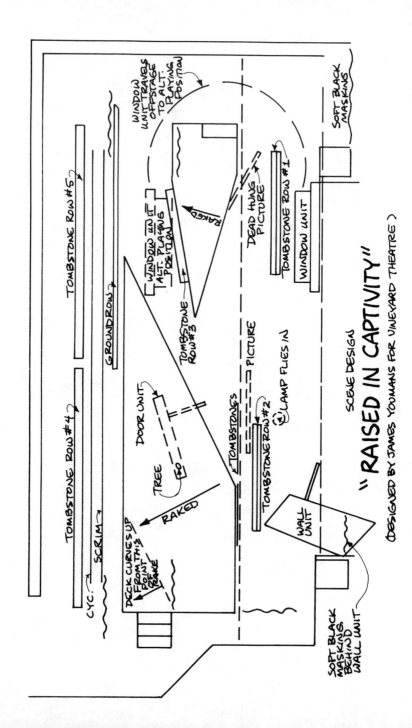

"RAISED IN CAPTIVITY"

(DESIGNED BY JAMES YOUMANS FOR VINEYARD THEATRE)

SCENE DESIGN

# NEW PLAYS

★ **THE EXONERATED by Jessica Blank and Erik Jensen.** Six interwoven stories paint a picture of an American criminal justice system gone horribly wrong and six brave souls who persevered to survive it. "The #1 play of the year...intense and deeply affecting..." *–NY Times.* "Riveting. Simple, honest storytelling that demands reflection." *–A.P.* "Artful and moving...pays tribute to the resilience of human hearts and minds." *–Variety.* "Stark...riveting...cunningly orchestrated." *–The New Yorker.* "Hard-hitting, powerful, and socially relevant." *–Hollywood Reporter.* [7M, 3W] ISBN: 0-8222-1946-8

★ **STRING FEVER by Jacquelyn Reingold.** Lily juggles the big issues: turning forty, artificial insemination and the elusive scientific Theory of Everything in this Off-Broadway comedy hit. "Applies the elusive rules of string theory to the conundrums of one woman's love life. Think *Sex and the City* meets *Copenhagen.*" *–NY Times.* "A funny offbeat and touching look at relationships...an appealing romantic comedy populated by oddball characters." *–NY Daily News.* "Where kooky, zany, and madcap meet...whimsically winsome." *–NY Magazine.* "STRING FEVER will have audience members happily stringing along." *–TheaterMania.com.* "Reingold's language is surprising, inventive, and unique." *–nytheatre.com.* "...[a] whimsical comic voice." *–Time Out.* [3M, 3W (doubling)] ISBN: 0-8222-1952-2

★ **DEBBIE DOES DALLAS adapted by Erica Schmidt, composed by Andrew Sherman, conceived by Susan L. Schwartz.** A modern morality tale told as a comic musical of tragic proportions as the classic film is brought to the stage. "A scream! A saucy, tongue-in-cheek romp." *–The New Yorker.* "Hilarious! DEBBIE manages to have it all: beauty, brains and a great sense of humor!" *–Time Out.* "Shamelessly silly, shrewdly self-aware and proud of being naughty. Great fun!" *–NY Times.* "Racy and raucous, a lighthearted, fast-paced thoroughly engaging and hilarious send-up." *–NY Daily News.* [3M, 5W] ISBN: 0-8222-1955-7

★ **THE MYSTERY PLAYS by Roberto Aguirre-Sacasa.** Two interrelated one acts, loosely based on the tradition of the medieval mystery plays. "... stylish, spine-tingling...Mr. Aguirre-Sacasa uses standard tricks of horror stories, borrowing liberally from masters like Kafka, Lovecraft, Hitchock...But his mastery of the genre is his own...irresistible." *–NY Times.* "Undaunted by the special-effects limitations of theatre, playwright and *Marvel* comic-book writer Roberto Aguirre-Sacasa maps out some creepy twilight zones in THE MYSTERY PLAYS, an engaging, related pair of one acts...The theatre may rarely deliver shocks equivalent to, say, *Dawn of the Dead*, but Aguirre-Sacasa's work is fine compensation." *–Time Out.* [4M, 2W] ISBN: 0-8222-2038-5

★ **THE JOURNALS OF MIHAIL SEBASTIAN by David Auburn.** This epic one-man play spans eight tumultuous years and opens a uniquely personal window on the Romanian Holocaust and the Second World War. "Powerful." *–NY Times.* "[THE JOURNALS OF MIHAIL SEBASTIAN] allows us to glimpse the idiosyncratic effects of that awful history on one intelligent, pragmatic, recognizably real man..." *–NY Newsday.* [3M, 5W] ISBN: 0-8222-2006-7

★ **LIVING OUT by Lisa Loomer.** The story of the complicated relationship between a Salvadoran nanny and the Anglo lawyer she works for. "A stellar new play. Searingly funny." *–The New Yorker.* "Both generous and merciless, equally enjoyable and disturbing." *–NY Newsday.* "A bitingly funny new comedy. The plight of working mothers is explored from two pointedly contrasting perspectives in this sympathetic, sensitive new play." *–Variety.* [2M, 6W] ISBN: 0-8222-1994-8

**DRAMATISTS PLAY SERVICE, INC.**
440 Park Avenue South, New York, NY 10016  212-683-8960  Fax 212-213-1539
postmaster@dramatists.com  www.dramatists.com

# NEW PLAYS

★ **MATCH by Stephen Belber.** Mike and Lisa Davis interview a dancer and choreographer about his life, but it is soon evident that their agenda will either ruin or inspire them—and definitely change their lives forever. "Prolific laughs and ear-to-ear smiles." *–NY Magazine.* "Uproariously funny, deeply moving, enthralling theater. Stephen Belber's MATCH has great beauty and tenderness, and abounds in wit." *–NY Daily News.* "Three and a half out of four stars." *–USA Today.* "A theatrical steeplechase that leads straight from outrageous bitchery to unadorned, heartfelt emotion." *–Wall Street Journal.* [2M, 1W] ISBN: 0-8222-2020-2

★ **HANK WILLIAMS: LOST HIGHWAY by Randal Myler and Mark Harelik.** The story of the beloved and volatile country-music legend Hank Williams, featuring twenty-five of his most unforgettable songs. "[LOST HIGHWAY has] the exhilarating feeling of Williams on stage in a particular place on a particular night...serves up classic country with the edges raw and the energy hot...By the end of the play, you've traveled on a profound emotional journey: LOST HIGHWAY transports its audience and communicates the inspiring message of the beauty and richness of Williams' songs...forceful, clear-eyed, moving, impressive." *–Rolling Stone.* "...honors a very particular musical talent with care and energy... smart, sweet, poignant." *–NY Times.* [7M, 3W] ISBN: 0-8222-1985-9

★ **THE STORY by Tracey Scott Wilson.** An ambitious black newspaper reporter goes against her editor to investigate a murder and finds the *best* story...but at what cost? "A singular new voice...deeply emotional, deeply intellectual, and deeply musical..." *–The New Yorker.* "...a conscientious and absorbing new drama..." *–NY Times.* "...a riveting, tough-minded drama about race, reporting and the truth..." *–A.P.* "... a stylish, attention-holding script that ends on a chilling note that will leave viewers with much to talk about." *–Curtain Up.* [2M, 7W (doubling, flexible casting)] ISBN: 0-8222-1998-0

★ **OUR LADY OF 121st STREET by Stephen Adly Guirgis.** The body of Sister Rose, beloved Harlem nun, has been stolen, reuniting a group of life-challenged childhood friends who square off as they wait for her return. "A scorching and dark new comedy... Mr. Guirgis has one of the finest imaginations for dialogue to come along in years." *–NY Times.* "Stephen Guirgis may be the best playwright in America under forty." *–NY Magazine.* [8M, 4W] ISBN: 0-8222-1965-4

★ **HOLLYWOOD ARMS by Carrie Hamilton and Carol Burnett.** The coming-of-age story of a dreamer who manages to escape her bleak life and follow her romantic ambitions to stardom. Based on Carol Burnett's bestselling autobiography, *One More Time.* "...pure theatre and pure entertainment..." *–Talkin' Broadway.* "...a warm, fuzzy evening of theatre." *–BrodwayBeat.com.* "...chuckles and smiles of recognition or surprise flow naturally...a remarkable slice of life." *–TheatreScene.net.* [5M, 5W, 1 girl] ISBN: 0-8222-1959-X

★ **INVENTING VAN GOGH by Steven Dietz.** A haunting and hallucinatory drama about the making of art, the obsession to create and the fine line that separates truth from myth. "Like a van Gogh painting, Dietz's story is a gorgeous example of excess—one that remakes reality with broad, well-chosen brush strokes. At evening's end, we're left with the author's resounding opinions on art and artifice, and provoked by his constant query into which is greater: van Gogh's art or his violent myth." *–Phoenix New Times.* "Dietz's writing is never simple. It is always brilliant. Shaded, compressed, direct, lucid—he frames his subject with a remarkable understanding of painting as a physical experience." *–Tucson Citizen.* [4M, 1W] ISBN: 0-8222-1954-9

**DRAMATISTS PLAY SERVICE, INC.**
**440 Park Avenue South, New York, NY 10016  212-683-8960  Fax 212-213-1539**
**postmaster@dramatists.com   www.dramatists.com**

# NEW PLAYS

★ **INTIMATE APPAREL by Lynn Nottage.** The moving and lyrical story of a turn-of-the-century black seamstress whose gifted hands and sewing machine are the tools she uses to fashion her dreams from the whole cloth of her life's experiences. "...Nottage's play has a delicacy and eloquence that seem absolutely right for the time she is depicting..." *–NY Daily News.* "...thoughtful, affecting...The play offers poignant commentary on an era when the cut and color of one's dress—and of course, skin—determined whom one could and could not marry, sleep with, even talk to in public." *–Variety.* [2M, 4W] ISBN: 0-8222-2009-1

★ **BROOKLYN BOY by Donald Margulies.** A witty and insightful look at what happens to a writer when his novel hits the bestseller list. "The characters are beautifully drawn, the dialogue sparkles..." *–nytheatre.com.* "Few playwrights have the mastery to smartly investigate so much through a laugh-out-loud comedy that combines the vintage subject matter of successful writer-returning-to-ethnic-roots with the familiar mid-life crisis." *–Show Business Weekly.* [4M, 3W] ISBN: 0-8222-2074-1

★ **CROWNS by Regina Taylor.** Hats become a springboard for an exploration of black history and identity in this celebratory musical play. "Taylor pulls off a Hat Trick: She scores thrice, turning CROWNS into an artful amalgamation of oral history, fashion show, and musical theater..." *–TheatreMania.com.* "...wholly theatrical...Ms. Taylor has created a show that seems to arise out of spontaneous combustion, as if a bevy of department-store customers simultaneously decided to stage a revival meeting in the changing room." *–NY Times.* [1M, 6W (2 musicians)] ISBN: 0-8222-1963-8

★ **EXITS AND ENTRANCES by Athol Fugard.** The story of a relationship between a young playwright on the threshold of his career and an aging actor who has reached the end of his. "[Fugard] can say more with a single line than most playwrights convey in an entire script...Paraphrasing the title, it's safe to say this drama, making its memorable entrance into our consciousness, is unlikely to exit as long as a theater exists for exceptional work." *–Variety.* "A thought-provoking, elegant and engrossing new play..." *–Hollywood Reporter.* [2M] ISBN: 0-8222-2041-5

★ **BUG by Tracy Letts.** A thriller featuring a pair of star-crossed lovers in an Oklahoma City motel facing a bug invasion, paranoia, conspiracy theories and twisted psychological motives. "...obscenely exciting...top-flight craftsmanship. Buckle up and brace yourself..." *–NY Times.* "...[a] thoroughly outrageous and thoroughly entertaining play...the possibility of enemies, real and imagined, to squash has never been more theatrical." *–A.P.* [3M, 2W] ISBN: 0-8222-2016-4

★ **THOM PAIN (BASED ON NOTHING) by Will Eno.** An ordinary man muses on childhood, yearning, disappointment and loss, as he draws the audience into his last-ditch plea for empathy and enlightenment. "It's one of those treasured nights in the theater—treasured nights anywhere, for that matter—that can leave you both breathless with exhilaration and...in a puddle of tears." *–NY Times.* "Eno's words...are familiar, but proffered in a way that is constantly contradictory to our expectations. Beckett is certainly among his literary ancestors." *–nytheatre.com.* [1M] ISBN: 0-8222-2076-8

★ **THE LONG CHRISTMAS RIDE HOME by Paula Vogel.** Past, present and future collide on a snowy Christmas Eve for a troubled family of five. "...[a] lovely and hauntingly original family drama...a work that breathes so much life into the theater." *–Time Out.* "...[a] delicate visual feast..." *–NY Times.* "...brutal and lovely...the overall effect is magical." *–NY Newsday.* [3M, 3W] ISBN: 0-8222-2003-2

**DRAMATISTS PLAY SERVICE, INC.**
**440 Park Avenue South, New York, NY 10016   212-683-8960   Fax 212-213-1539**
**postmaster@dramatists.com   www.dramatists.com**